AN ESSENTIAL GUIDE TO

W9-DBO-032

spiritual

gifts

Ron Phillips

CHARISMA
HOUSE

Most CHARISMA HOUSE BOOK GROUP products are available at special quantity discounts for bulk purchase for sales promotions, premiums, fund-raising, and educational needs. For details, write Charisma House Book Group, 600 Rinehart Road, Lake Mary, Florida 32746, or telephone (407) 333-0600.

AN ESSENTIAL GUIDE TO SPIRITUAL GIFTS by
  Ron Phillips
Published by Charisma House
Charisma Media/Charisma House Book Group
600 Rinehart Road
Lake Mary, Florida 32746
www.charismahouse.com

Unless otherwise noted, all Scripture quotations are from the New King James Version of the Bible. Copyright © 1979, 1980, 1982 by Thomas Nelson, Inc., publishers. Used by permission.

Scripture quotations marked AKJV are from the American King James Version. Public domain.

Scripture quotations marked AMP are from the Amplified Bible. Old Testament copyright © 1965, 1987 by the Zondervan Corporation. The Amplified New Testament copyright © 1954, 1958, 1987 by the Lockman Foundation. Used by permission.

Scripture quotations marked ASV are from the American Standard Version of the Bible.

Scripture quotations marked KJV are from the King James Version of the Bible.

Scripture quotations marked NIV are from the Holy Bible, New International Version. Copyright © 1973, 1978, 1984, International Bible Society. Used by permission.

Cover design by Justin Evans

Design Director: Bill Johnson

Visit the author's website at www.ronphillips.org.

Library of Congress Cataloging-in-Publication Data:
  Phillips, Ron M.
  An essential guide to spiritual gifts / Ron Phillips. -- 1st ed.
      p. cm.
  Includes bibliographical references (p.   ).
  ISBN 978-1-61638-493-7 (trade paper) -- ISBN 978-1-61638-631-3 (e-book) 1. Gifts, Spiritual. I. Title.
  BT767.3.P55 2012
  234'.13--dc23

                                            2011044557

While the author has made every effort to provide accurate telephone numbers and Internet addresses at the time of publication, neither the publisher nor the author assumes any responsibility for errors or for changes that occur after publication.

First Edition

12 13 14 15 16 — 987654321

Printed in the United States of America

CONTENTS

CHAPTER ONE

The Gifts of the Holy Spirit: Their Need and Purpose

ARLY IN HIS career, Thomas Edison—the genius inventor who would come to be known as the "Wizard of Menlo Park"—invented an electric voting machine. While working at the newsstand on the Port Huron to Detroit railroad, Edison had read copious articles that detailed the long and laborious process Congress had in voting on any and every issue. These delays often inhibited the ability of Congress to create or deal with needed and helpful legislation. Clearly, they needed a way to make the process less time consuming and more efficient. Enter Thomas Edison and his electric voting machine.[1]

The machine Edison had invented enabled the congressman to flip a switch to the right or left and cast a vote without leaving his desk. This eliminated the tedium of ballot preparation, marking, waiting in line to drop the ballot into the ballot box, the delay of forward motion while waiting for the ballots to be counted, and so on. Edison obtained a patent on this device (it was his first) and traveled to Washington to meet with a congressional representative.

At the demonstration of Edison's invention, the congressman praised Edison's ingenuity and vision. Nevertheless, the congressman promptly turned down the device saying, "Filibustering and delay in the tabulation of votes are often the only means we have for defeating bad or improper legislation."

Edison was, understandably, crushed. The invention was good; he was certain of this not only from his own part, but also due to the praise of the congressman. The invention would help to eliminate the delays that so often led to the inability of Congress to function at maximum efficiency. The invention was needed; it just wasn't wanted.

Many Christians today live the same way. They believe in the atoning work of Jesus, and they endeavor to have a relationship with God that is real and full. The Holy Spirit and the subsequent gifts His presence brings would benefit their lives immeasurably, but they believe those gifts were for another time or that their relationship with God is good enough as it is. The supernatural gifts of the Holy Spirit are needed, but they aren't wanted.

Who Is the Holy Spirit?

Many people view the Holy Spirit as a tangential member of the Trinity. God the Father, they say, is God, certainly, and it almost goes without saying that Jesus is also God. The Holy Spirit, however, is an enigmatic, ephemeral entity. To some, the Holy Spirit is an indwelling force that descends from God Himself to guide the believer in every conceivable action and decision; to others, the Holy Spirit is a life-giving same spirit that raised Christ from the dead (Rom. 8:11) that enables them to live in a particular way; yet still to others, the Holy Spirit is akin to a Jiminy Cricket–like conscience figure sitting on their shoulders and helping them to live "good lives." This lack of clarity was dealt with early on in church history.

The early church had to deal with multiplicities of understandings and disparate teachings regarding the Holy Spirit in His person, role, and function. In addressing these issues, the First Council of Constantinople at Nicaea in 381 established the following section of the Nicene Creed stating as a *credo*:

> [We Believe] in the Holy Spirit, the Lord and Giver of life; who proceedeth from the Father and Son, who with the Father and the Son is worshipped and glorified...

The Holy Spirit, according to this council, is one with the Father and the Son. The Holy Spirit is to be worshiped. The Holy Spirit, then, is God just as much as is the Father and Jesus, the Son.

The Holy Spirit in Creation

Before there was anything, which is to say "at the beginning of everything" when God created the heavens and the earth, we're told that the Holy Spirit moved over the face of the deep:

> In the beginning God created the heavens and the earth. And the earth was waste and void; and darkness was upon the face of the deep: and the Spirit of God moved upon the face of the waters.
>
> —Genesis 1:1–2, ASV

Here is God, the Holy Spirit, hovering over a semblance of the earth that was to come—a chaotic wellspring of God's creation. This word *moved* is the Hebrew word *rachaph*, which means "to flutter or brood." This same word is used only two more times in the Bible. It's used in Deuteronomy 32:9–12 as follows:

> For Jehovah's portion is his people; Jacob is the lot of his inheritance. He found him in a desert land, and in the waste howling wilderness; he compassed him about, he cared for him, he kept him as the apple of his eye. As an eagle stirreth up her nest, that *fluttereth* over her young, he spread abroad his wings, he took them, He bare them on his pinions. Jehovah alone did lead him, and there was no foreign god with him.
>
> —ASV, EMPHASIS ADDED

And in Jeremiah 23:9:

> Concerning the prophets. My heart within me is broken, all my bones *shake*; I am like a drunken

man, and like a man whom wine has overcome, because of Jehovah, and because of his holy words.

—ASV, EMPHASIS ADDED

In these passages we get a glimpse of the overwhelming, orderly, and even motherly nature of the Holy Spirit. Additionally, we read in Hebrews 11:3 that God's Word brought all of creation into existence by the power of His Holy Spirit:[2]

By faith we understand that the worlds have been framed by the word of God, so that what is seen hath not been made out of things which appear.

—HEBREWS 11:3, ASV

Clearly, the Holy Spirit is active in the birth of all life on Planet Earth. The Holy Spirit is God's life released on the chaotic, flooded earth.

The Holy Spirit in the creation of man

It is evident that the Holy Spirit worked to create order out of the chaos present at the beginning, but in Genesis 2:7 we read the following amazing words:

And Jehovah God formed man of the dust of the ground, and breathed into his nostrils the breath of life; and man became a living soul.

—ASV

God "breathed" into man to give him life. The word *breathed* is *naphach* in Hebrew, which comes from *nephesh* or "soul." God's Spirit gave a "soul" to man.

Theologian Wayne Grudem in his classic work *Systematic Theology* defines the work of the Holy Spirit as follows: "The work of the Holy Spirit is to manifest the active presence of God in the world and especially in the church."[3]

The Holy Spirit in the creation of Scripture

It is not simply important but vital to understand that the Holy Spirit also inspired the sacred Scriptures, both Old and New Testament. For example, in 2 Peter 1:19–21:

> And we have the prophetic word [made] firmer still. You will do well to pay close attention to it as to a lamp shining in a dismal (squalid and dark) place, until the day breaks through [the gloom] and the Morning Star rises (comes into being) in your hearts. [Yet] first [you must] understand this, that no prophecy of Scripture is [a matter] of any personal or private or special interpretation (loosening, solving). For no prophecy ever originated because some man willed it [to do so—it never came by human impulse], but men spoke from God who were borne along (moved and impelled) by the Holy Spirit.
>
> —AMP

This idea of the writers of the Bible being "borne along by the Holy Spirit" is a beautiful word picture. Peter explains to the reader, using nautical terms with which he would have been familiar, the process through which the writers received inspiration.

Imagine the Sea of Galilee. Now picture a solitary fishing boat sitting out on a calm sea. Suddenly the wind begins to move and the sails begin to billow. The wind fills the sail and begins to move the boat swiftly through the water. It is in this way that the Holy Spirit filled the writers of the Bible to convey the narratives, truths, and prophecies that God wished to convey to the generations.

The Holy Spirit and Jesus

This book is being written in the months just prior to Christmas, and it is only natural that my mind turns to what is a most wondrous work of the Holy Spirit: the Incarnation.

In the rugged plain of Esdralon in Judea sits the little town of Nazareth. A young girl named Mary, probably a teenager, works diligently for the proliferation and sustenance of her family. She is innocent, barely of the age to consider marriage. A carpenter named Joseph meets with Mary's father to ask for her hand in marriage. The engagement is set, and, for all intents and purposes, in the eyes of their community they are married, though they do not live together and have not consummated their marriage.

One night Mary's peaceful sleep is disturbed by an

angel named Gabriel who came to her with a startling declaration:

> And having come in, the angel said to her, "Rejoice, highly favored one, the Lord is with you; blessed are you among women!" But when she saw him, she was troubled at his saying, and considered what manner of greeting this was. Then the angel said to her, "Do not be afraid, Mary, for you have found favor with God. And behold, you will conceive in your womb and bring forth a Son, and shall call His name Jesus. He will be great, and will be called the Son of the Highest; and the Lord God will give Him the throne of His father David. And He will reign over the house of Jacob forever, and of His kingdom there will be no end."
>
> —LUKE 1:28–33

Imagine being in Mary's position. She has just received news she is to be the mother of the Messiah. Her simple response, "How can this be, since I do not know a man?" is answered with an astounding revelation by Gabriel:

> The Holy Spirit will come upon you, and the power of the Highest will overshadow you; therefore, also, that Holy One who is to be born will be called Son of God.... For with God nothing will be impossible.
>
> —LUKE 1:35–37

Jesus was conceived in Mary's virgin womb by the power and "overshadowing" of the Holy Spirit!

Before leaving this account, it might do us some good to take a look at another aspect of this narrative.

We're told in Ephesians 2:8 that faith is not something that humans have inherently or even that it is something that we choose to believe, but, rather, faith is a gift to us from God:

> For by grace you have been saved through faith, and that not of yourselves; it is the gift of God.

Now, place yourself in Mary's (and even Joseph's) position. You've just been told, separately from your betrothed, that a thing never before imagined outside of the realm of prophets—whom are never without honor except in their own country—is about to happen: a virgin is going to bear a child. What manner of faith must have been required on Mary's part? We might easily dismiss this since Mary would have firsthand knowledge of her lack of sexual experience, and the moment she begins to show the physical signs of pregnancy she has then moved from faith to evidence. But what about Joseph?

Imagine the tremendous gift of faith that must have been given to Joseph: to hear the word of one who appeared in a dream and believe it enough to not put Mary away privately—as he almost did to save her from disgrace—or to shame her publicly—as was his right—and thereby probably cause her death!

The soft glow of that particular Christmas miracle—the miracle of faith given to Mary and Joseph—has often been outshined by the brilliance of the miracle of the Incarnation, but to leave this account and not see the miraculous work of the Holy Spirit in the life of the earthly parents of our Lord would be a woeful loss on our part. Thank God for the miracle faith brought on by the power of His Holy Spirit!

The Holy Spirit in the Ministry of Jesus

Before tackling the topics in this section, it's important to clarify a few important doctrinal issues regarding the person of Jesus. This is not meant to be exhaustive as there is a wealth of material available for the study of Christology; however, it must be stated at the outset that Jesus was both fully God and fully man. Though He retained His deity through His manhood, it is important—especially within the auspices of this book's subject—to note that Jesus, as God in the flesh, chose to divest Himself from the independent use of His power as God. He was, instead, ever led by God the Holy Spirit in the use of His godly attributes.

Jesus Christ operated as Spirit-filled man while on the earth. He never surrendered His deity during the days of His flesh, yet He emptied Himself of the prerogatives of deity and operated in the power of the Holy Spirit.

> Let this mind be in you, which was also in Christ Jesus: who, being in the form of God, thought it not robbery to be equal with God: but made himself of no reputation, and took upon him the form of a servant, and was made in the likeness of men: and being found in fashion as a man, he humbled himself, and became obedient unto death, even the death of the cross.
>
> —Philippians 2:5–8, kjv

Jesus emptied Himself and became an example of the Spirit-filled life. At His water baptism Jesus was filled with the Holy Spirit. Consider the account in Luke 3:21–22:

> When all the people were baptized, it came to pass that Jesus also was baptized; and while He prayed, the heaven was opened. And the Holy Spirit descended in bodily form like a dove upon Him, and a voice came from heaven which said, "You are My beloved Son; in You I am well pleased."

And in Luke 4:1–2:

> Then Jesus, being filled with the Holy Spirit, returned from the Jordan and was led by the Spirit into the wilderness, being tempted for forty days by the devil. And in those days He ate nothing, and afterward, when they had ended, He was hungry.

The Holy Spirit in the baptism of Jesus

It is approximately thirty years since the Annunciation, and a wild man who dresses in camel skins and eats locusts dipped in honey has set up for revival on the banks of the Jordan River near Bethany. His message was a simple one: REPENT! John's message of repentance was couched in the broader message of the soon appearance of God's Messiah, the one whose laces John would not be fit to tie. John told his listeners:

> I indeed baptize you with water; but One mightier than I is coming, whose sandal strap I am not worthy to loose. He will baptize you with the Holy Spirit and fire. His winnowing fan is in His hand, and He will thoroughly clean out His threshing floor, and gather the wheat into His barn; but the chaff He will burn with unquenchable fire.
>
> —LUKE 3:16–27

One day, mid-sermon, Jesus appeared there on the banks of the Jordan; this sinless man had hearkened to John's message of repentance. But the appearance of Jesus was met with jubilation by John:

> Behold! The Lamb of God who takes away the sin of the world! This is He of whom I said, "After me comes a Man who is preferred before me, for He before me." I did not know Him; but that He should be revealed to Israel, therefore I have come baptizing with water.
>
> —JOHN 1:29–31

Now imagine the face of this Baptist when Jesus entered the cool waters of the Jordan and placed Himself before John for baptism. Read his words:

> I need to be baptized by You, and are You coming to me?
>
> —MATTHEW 3:14

John was acknowledging the fact that Jesus had no need of repentance. But Jesus showed profound humility in His obedience to God. Even though He was perfect and pure, He was, in the words of Matthew Henry regarding John 17:19, "washed as if he had been polluted; and thus for our sakes he sanctified himself, that we also might be sanctified, and be baptized with him."[4]

Jesus responded to John's declaration by displaying His absolute obedience to the will of God the Father:

> Permit it to be so now, for thus it is fitting for us to fulfill all righteousness.
>
> —MATTHEW 3:15

Even though Jesus was fully God and had never sinned, He demonstrated the willful divestment of His godly attributes.

Now picture yourself in the crowd gathered there on the Jordan's sandy banks. You see John lower Jesus into the water, and as Jesus stands, the heavens open and a figure that has taken the appearance of a dove—the Holy

Spirit—begins to descend from the skies, and suddenly a voice sounds from the vastness saying:

> This is My beloved Son, in whom I am well pleased.
> —Matthew 3:17

This, most suggest, is the beginning of the earthly ministry of Jesus. How wonderful it is to see that Jesus would not begin His ministry, nor dare to endure the trials of it, without the assistance and empowerment of the Holy Spirit. And speaking of trials...

After His baptism, Jesus was led by the Holy Spirit into the desert wilderness where He fasted for forty days and nights and was tempted by Satan. Jesus thwarted the temptation of Satan and came out of His wilderness fast in the power of the Holy Spirit. His formal announcement of the beginning of His ministry was steeped in a controversial pronouncement:

> "The *Spirit of the Lord* is upon Me, because He has anointed Me to preach the gospel to the poor; He has sent Me to heal the brokenhearted, to proclaim liberty to the captives and recovery of sight to the blind, to set at liberty those who are oppressed; to proclaim the acceptable year of the Lord."
>
> Then He closed the book, and gave it back to the attendant and sat down. And the eyes of all who were in the synagogue were fixed on Him. And He began to say to them, "Today this Scripture is fulfilled in your hearing."
> —Luke 4:18–21, emphasis added

If Jesus—God incarnate, the fullness of the God-man—needed the Holy Spirit, then obviously all believers have a greater need!

The Holy Spirit in Conversion

In the Shema, the great commandment given to Israel in the desert, we are told to "love the LORD [our] God with all [our] heart, with all [our] soul, and with all [our] strength" (Deut. 6:4–5). I have heard many preachers, teachers, and Christian apologists use this instruction, and Jesus's affirmation of it, to advance the notion that Christianity is a logical faith that can withstand scrutiny and questioning. I do believe this, however; to make Christianity about the mind only is a dangerous path to tread. Christianity does stand up to reason, and a person should give serious consideration to any idea preached from a pulpit, but there is more to the experience and process of conversion. A. W. Tozer, the great evangelist and one of the most insightful writers of the twentieth century, affirmed the following precept in his book *The Mystery of the Holy Spirit*:

> If you have to be reasoned into Christianity, some wise fellow can reason you out of it! If you come to Christ by a flash of the Holy Spirit so that by intuition you know that you are God's child, you know it by the text but you also know it by the inner light, the inner illumination of the Spirit, and no one can ever reason you out of it.[5]

Don't misunderstand; this idea is not unique to Tozer. His proclamation is merely an elaboration and explanation of a very simple yet vital biblical truth taught by Jesus in John 16:8–15 as He, Jesus, attempted to explain the work of the coming Comforter to His disciples:

> And when [the Holy Spirit] has come, He will convict the world of sin, and of righteousness, and of judgment: of sin, because they do not believe in Me; of righteousness, because I go to My Father and you see Me no more; of judgment, because the ruler of this world is judged. I still have many things to say to you, but you cannot bear them now. However, when He, the Spirit of truth, has come, He will guide you into all truth; for He will not speak on His own authority, but whatever He hears He will speak; and He will tell you things to come. He will glorify Me, for He will take of what is Mine and declare it to you. All things that the Father has are Mine. Therefore I said that [the Holy Spirit] will take of Mine and declare it to you.

In a previous book in this series, I detailed the implications of the conversation between Jesus and Nicodemus wherein Jesus explained to the Pharisee that a birth from above by the Spirit was necessary to enter the kingdom of God:

> Most assuredly, I say to you, unless one is born of water and the Spirit, he cannot enter the kingdom

of God. That which is born of the flesh is flesh, and that which is born of the Spirit is spirit. Do not marvel that I said to you, "You must be born again." The wind blows where it wishes, and you hear the sound of it, but cannot tell where it comes from and where it goes. So is everyone who is born of the Spirit.

—John 3:5–8

When you combine these three teachings, you start to get a picture of the truth that our new life comes to us by virtue of the Spirit and not, in fact, by anything or any work in which we might trust. In one of the hardest times of the ministry of Jesus, He was forced to watch as many disciples turned away because His teaching had become "hard saying[s]." To this, Jesus responded as follows:

It is the Spirit who gives life; the flesh profits nothing. The words that I speak to you are spirit, and they are life.

—John 6:63

Hear those words; the Spirit is life! At conversion the spirit of a person is made alive by the Holy Spirit. The living soul of a person indwelled by the Holy Spirit is the miracle of salvation.

The Holy Spirit in the Church

Again, although limited by space, I want to briefly note some biblical evidences of the Holy Spirit's work in the lives of believers.

This same Holy Spirit that filled Jesus, empowered His ministry, and raised Him from the dead releases the baptism with the Holy Spirit, which establishes a power connection to the spiritual dimension. (See my book *An Essential Guide to Baptism of the Holy Spirit.*) It's as John said in Luke 3:16 to those gathered on the banks of the Jordan:

> John answered, saying to all, "I indeed baptize you with water; but One mightier than I is coming, whose sandal strap I am not worthy to loose. He will baptize you with the Holy Spirit and fire."

The Holy Spirit also birthed the church on the Day of Pentecost in fulfillment of prophecy (Joel 2), as we read in Acts 2:1–4:

> When the Day of Pentecost had fully come, they were all with one accord in one place. And suddenly there came a sound from heaven, as of a rushing mighty wind, and it filled the whole house where they were sitting. Then there appeared to them divided tongues, as of fire, and one sat upon each of them. And they were all filled with the Holy Spirit and began to speak with other tongues, as the Spirit gave them utterance.

And in Acts 2:33:

> Therefore being exalted to the right hand of God,
> and having received from the Father the promise
> of the Holy Spirit, He poured out this which you
> now see and hear.

The Holy Spirit performed miracles in the early church,
empowering all they did. The writer of Hebrews was clear
in acknowledging the source of that power:

> ...God also bearing witness both with signs and
> wonders, with various miracles, and gifts of the
> Holy Spirit, according to His own will?
> —HEBREWS 2:4

The Holy Spirit cleansed the early church and brought
His fruit into their lives to sanctify them.

> But the fruit of the Spirit is love, joy, peace, long-
> suffering, kindness, goodness, faithfulness, gen-
> tleness, self-control. Against such there is no law.
> And those who are Christ's have crucified the flesh
> with its passions and desires. If we live in the Spirit,
> let us also walk in the Spirit.
> —GALATIANS 5:22–25

The Holy Spirit empowered their witness and gave
them great boldness to win others to faith in Christ. The

Holy Spirit brings a transforming atmosphere of love and joy when He is welcomed.

> Now hope does not disappoint, because the love of God has been poured out in our hearts by the Holy Spirit who was given to us.
>
> —Romans 5:5

> For the kingdom of God is not eating and drinking, but righteousness and peace and joy in the Holy Spirit.
>
> —Romans 14:17

If diligently pursed by believers, this atmosphere produces a genuine unity among believers in the church. As we are admonished in Ephesians 4:3–6:

> [Endeavor] to keep the unity of the Spirit in the bond of peace. There is one body and one Spirit, just as you were called in one hope of your calling; one Lord, one faith, one baptism; one God and Father of all, who is above all, and through all, and in you all.

Finally, the Holy Spirit equips believers by bestowing the gifts of the Spirit. This was Jesus's ascension promise to His disciples.

The Holy Spirit is to be adored and worshiped as God the Father and Son are on the earth. He must not be feared or ignored!

Great is the Father
Great is the Son
Great is the Holy Ghost
Three in One
Jehovah is His name.

—Author Unknown

Praise God from whom all blessings flow
Praise Him all creatures here below
Praise Him above, ye Heavenly hosts
Praise Father, Son, and Holy Ghost.

—Doxology (public domain)

CHAPTER TWO

The Promise of the
Gifts of the Spirit

B EFORE OUR LORD Jesus Christ ascended to heaven,
He left a plan for the kingdom on Planet Earth.
Jesus left the church on earth.

Jesus was in Caesarea Philippi when the time came to
give a final exam to those whom He had mentored. Here
is the record of the powerful moment:

> When Jesus came into the region of Caesarea
> Philippi, He asked His disciples, saying, "Who
> do men say that I, the Son of Man, am?" So they
> said, "Some say John the Baptist, some Elijah, and
> others Jeremiah or one of the prophets." He said
> to them, "But who do you that say I am?" Simon
> Peter answered and said, "You are the Christ, the
> Son of the living God." Jesus answered and said
> to him, "Blessed are you, Simon Bar-Jonah, for
> flesh and blood has not revealed this to you, but
> My Father who is in heaven. And I also say to you
> that you are Peter, and on this rock I will build
> My church, and the gates of Hades shall not pre-
> vail against it. And I will give you the keys of the
> kingdom of heaven, and whatever you bind on

earth will be bound in heaven, and whatever you
loose on earth will be loosed in heaven."
—MATTHEW 16:13–19

This word *Christ* is the Greek word *Christos*, which
is a translation of the Hebrew word *mashiyach*, which is
where we get the word *Messiah*, which means, literally, an
anointed or consecrated person. Peter understood that
He, Jesus, was the Christ, the Messiah; this affirmation
released the powerful strategy of Jesus to go to the world
with the good news. Jesus would build a church. The
English word *church* translates from the Greek *ecclesia*,
which means "the called out and called together." Jesus
was assembling a core group who understood who He was
and what He had come to do. He promised that group
hell-defeating power and the keys to the spiritual realm to
accomplish their mission.

The disciples would stumble for a season when Jesus
was arrested, crucified, and buried. After Jesus's resurrection, they would rediscover faith and hope.

Power in the Great Commission

After His first days of post-resurrection appearance on
earth, Jesus led the disciples out to the Mount of Olives.
There, in front of five hundred eyewitnesses, Jesus gave the
Great Commission:

And Jesus came and spoke to them, saying, "All
authority has been given to Me in heaven and on

earth. Go therefore and make disciples of all the nations, baptizing them in the name of the Father and of the Son and of the Holy Spirit, teaching them to observe all things that I have commanded you; and lo, I am with you always, even to the end of the age." Amen.

—MATTHEW 28:18–20

Jesus left His church with a commission to go into all the world with His transforming message! He left this enormous assignment in the hands of 11 disciples and 109 others forming a group of 120!

Here is a church with a commission yet no visible resources. There was no wealth, no building, no governmental favor, and no religious support. Rather there were hostility and threats!

However, Jesus did not leave them completely empty-handed. He left them with one other asset: a promise. That promise was revealed in the Old Testament Scriptures in the book of the prophet Joel. A day was coming when the Holy Spirit, the third person of the Godhead, would be released on the earth in mighty power.

And it shall come to pass afterward that I will pour out My Spirit on all flesh; your sons and your daughters shall prophesy, your old men shall dream dreams, your young men shall see visions. And also on My menservants and on My maidservants I will pour out My Spirit in those days. And I

will show wonders in the heavens and in the earth:
Blood and fire and pillars of smoke. The sun shall
be turned into darkness, and the moon into blood,
before the coming of the great and awesome day of
the Lord. And it shall come to pass that whoever
calls on the name of the Lord shall be saved.

For in Mount Zion and in Jerusalem there shall
be deliverance, as the LORD has said, among the
remnant whom the LORD calls.

—JOEL 2:28–32

This strategic epoch would result in an outpouring of God that would touch all people regardless of age, background, race, or gender. This release would result in dreams, visions, and wonders. An age of miracles and wonders that would result in many calling on the Lord to be saved was coming. Jesus had hinted at this promise all throughout His three-year ministry, but on that day every prophecy was now dawning!

Living waters

In a move that would be soundly ridiculed by countless pastors and counselors today, Jesus once instructed His disciples to go search for food so He could spend some time alone at a well with a woman of less-than-savory moral fiber. However, this encounter was vital to this precious woman's recovery, deliverance, and salvation. It was in this discourse that Jesus first introduced the concept of the importance of the Holy Spirit to the Jews' estranged relatives, the Samaritans. Jesus's encounter with the wayward woman at the well was all about the promise of the Holy Spirit. This fallen woman was pronounced a new beginning and new inner power for a better life:

> Jesus answered and said to her, "Whoever drinks of this water will thirst again, but whoever drinks of the water that I shall give him will never thirst. But the water that I shall give him will become in him a fountain of water springing up into everlasting life."
>
> —JOHN 4:13–14

What was that "fountain" Jesus promised? Later at the Feast of Tabernacles Jesus gave another clue about this promise.

> On the last day, that great day of the feast, Jesus stood and cried out, saying, "If anyone thirsts, let him come to Me and drink. He who believes in Me, as the Scripture has said, out of his heart will flow rivers of living water." But this He spoke concerning the Spirit, whom those believing in Him would receive; for the Holy Spirit was not yet given, because Jesus was not yet glorified.
>
> —JOHN 7:37–39

Here He promises "rivers of living water." The beloved apostle John explains this promise to be the Holy Spirit as prophesied in Joel! Could the "rivers" mean different gifts or capacities that flow into a needy world?

Empowerment

In the Great Commission, the ones most in need are those being commissioned. After all, they are going out "as sheep among wolves." The disciples experienced a level of protection, certainly, while Jesus was with them here on the earth, but what were they to do once He was no longer among them physically? As Jesus moved toward the end of His earthly journey, He spoke of the "Helper."

> And I will pray the Father, and He will give you another Helper, that He may abide with you forever— the Spirit of truth, whom the world cannot receive, because it neither sees Him nor knows Him; but you know Him, for He dwells with you and will be in you. I will not leave you orphans; I will come to you.
> —JOHN 14:16–18

Notice the beauty in the promise of Jesus not to leave His followers as "orphans." The invisible God that the world cannot see was coming to "abide" with the church forever.

John 14:26 promises that "the Helper" would give teaching and revelation to the young church. John 15:26 promised "the Helper" would empower the church's witness to the Father and Son! In John 16:7–8 Jesus promised that "the Helper" would bring the abiding, convicting, and empowering presence of God for the church's mission.

In John 14:12–14 Jesus promises an age that will surpass all the miracles He performed on the earth. An age of "greater works" is clearly promised.

> Most assuredly, I say to you, he who believes in Me, the works that I do he will do also; and greater works than these he will do, because I go to My Father. And whatever you ask in My name, that I will do, that the Father may be glorified in the Son. If you ask anything in My name, I will do it.

Imagine that! The Lamb of God, who worked greater miracles than the world had ever seen—and we understand that it was He who created all things—promised that we, His church, would be enabled and empowered to do greater works than were seen done by Him. It should be plain that this work of the Holy Spirit to empower is very much needed in the life of *every* believer.

Making good on the promise

There is nothing I would not do for my children. I have loved them poorly at times, but God in His great goodness has helped to mend and restore those relationships. Even now at my advanced age, I still sometimes see them as little babes in my arms. Yet I know that as much as I love my children and as much as I would do anything for them that I could, when compared to God's love for

His children, my love is like hatred. Jesus explained this dynamic in Luke's Gospel:

> If a son asks for bread from any father among you, will he give him a stone? Or if he asks for a fish, will he give him a serpent instead of a fish? Or if he asks for an egg, will he offer him a scorpion? If you then, being evil, know how to give good gifts to your children, how much more will your heavenly Father give the Holy Spirit to those who ask Him!
> —LUKE 11:11–13

Luke's Gospel promises the Holy Spirit as a gift from the Father. It is Luke who records the clear promise to the disciples. First in Luke 24:49:

> Behold, I send the Promise of My Father upon you; but tarry in the city of Jerusalem until you are endued with power from on high.

And also in Acts 1:4–5:

> And being assembled together with them, He commanded them not to depart from Jerusalem, but to wait for the Promise of the Father, "which," He said, "you have heard from Me; for John truly baptized with water, but you shall be baptized with the Holy Spirit not many days from now."

Jesus's ascension promise was the gift of the Holy Spirit and His power without measure. Ten days later in the Upper Room on Mount Zion, the Holy Spirit was poured out during the Feast of Pentecost. In that place, Mount Zion—where David instituted and released thirty-three years of nonstop worship in a tabernacle, where the *shekinah* glory had dwelt in the temple, where Jesus had broken bread and given the cup of wine to establish the New Covenant with the church, and in that place where the blood covenant was made—Jesus birthed the early church in the power of the Holy Spirit.

In that experience there are early flashes of spiritual gifts such as tongues, miraculous signs, and gifts of utterance and understanding. This powerful moment took the church from 120 to 3,120 in less than an hour! The newborn church had its beginning in the gift and giftings of the Holy Spirit.

Psalm 68:18 prophesied that at Jesus's ascension He would receive gifts to be used among men. Paul would cite this psalm in Ephesians 4:7–12. When our Lord ascended on high and presented the blood upon the altar of glory, He received the gift *and gifts* of the Spirit from the Father for the church! Jesus poured out the Holy Spirit on His new body the church without limit or measure. Look at these verses in Psalm 68:

> You have ascended on high, You have led captivity captive; You have received gifts among men, even from the rebellious, that the LORD God might

> dwell there. Blessed be the LORD, who daily loads
> us with benefits, the God of our salvation! Selah.
> —PSALM 68:18–19

Notice in verse 19, He promised to "daily [load] us with benefits." This is a prophecy of the bestowing of the gifts of the Spirit. One interesting thing to note is that the word *benefits* is not in the Hebrew. The text simply says of God that "He daily loads us…" The gifts are His daily endowment for the church.

What Has Become of the Gifted Church?

Since Jesus commissioned the church and sent the enablement, why hasn't the church completed her commission?

The reason, I think, is that the church operates in so little power and so much carnality in the absence of the true operation of the gifts of the Spirit. Some say these endowments have ceased. They say that the gifts are no longer needed or valid. They believe the church can operate on its intellect, ingenuity, marketing strategy, and lukewarm commitment. This must change if the church is to experience true renewal. The church life needs the transformation of Pentecostal gifting and power.

> Repent, and let every one of you be baptized in
> the name of Jesus Christ for the remission of sins;
> and you shall receive the gift of the Holy Spirit.
> For the promise is to you and to your children,

and to all who are afar off, as many as the Lord
our God will call.

—Acts 2:39

This verse declares that the promised Spirit and His
gifts are for all the church for all times! This book will be
an effort at recovery of "the promise."

CHAPTER THREE

The Availability of the Gifts of the Spirit Today

CAN A THEOLOGY that includes certain *charismata* or "gifts" be biblical? Furthermore, can such practices be included in the family of churches? I believe that the answer to the first is a resounding yes. I also hope that there can be a positive answer to the second statement. So, the question arises: Is there room at the evangelical table for those of us who practice what is commonly referred to as the charismatic gifts, primarily that of speaking in tongues?*

Evangelicals were not birthed in the high halls of academia but from the contexts of ecclesiastical dissent and enthusiastic revivalism. The roots of evangelicals were laid down in the Great Awakening with all of its spiritual passion. Only in recent generations have evangelicals sought to shake the hayseed of the brush arbor from our hair and embrace the scholasticism that bows at the altar of the human mind rather than the sovereign Spirit of God.

The results have been disastrous. We have moved from emphasis on the inerrancy of Scripture. Many sincere

---

* Materials in this chapter are drawn from research from previous books and articles by Dr. Phillips.

Christians who hold to the continuation of certain spiritual gifts have been marginalized by leadership of their respective denominations.

Unfortunately, our approach has been to attempt to confront a pagan world with merely an intellectual appreciation of the Scriptures. The idea that one can confront the militant passion of Islamic terrorists with just a convincing argument is somewhat naïve. As the great apostle Paul said:

> When I came to you, [I] did not come with excellence of speech or of wisdom declaring to you the testimony of God. For I determined not to know anything among you except Jesus Christ and Him crucified. I was with you in weakness, in fear, and in much trembling. And my speech and my preaching were not with persuasive words of human wisdom, but in demonstration of the Spirit and of power, that your faith should not be in the wisdom of men but in the power of God.
>
> —1 CORINTHIANS 2:1–5

To the end that we recover not simply the doctrine of the Holy Spirit but His presence and power overrides any thought of winning an argument. We are sending forth a generation who does not know how to cast out devils and, like the sons of Sceva, they are being chased out of the ministry. (See Acts 19:13–16.)

God, through the gifts of the Spirit, allows us to

experience the power of the world to come. In the present operation of the gifts, we have a dimensional break-through from God's throne to this present world. The reality of the presence and power of the Spirit is simply a down payment of glory from that deathless world to come! God's kingdom, though coming, is already present in His people through the Holy Spirit. At conversion, the kingdom breaks through to give a spiritual birth. The gift of the precious Holy Spirit releases gifts to His body—the church—to demonstrate that the kingdom has broken through into this present world.

This affirms the present availability and operation of charismatic gifts. I further affirm that evangelicals need not fear those who embrace the gifts, but they should welcome them. In doing so, evangelicals welcome the third person of the Godhead, the Holy Spirit.

Biblical Support for the Continuation of Charismatic Gifts

Those who believe the gifts have ceased have virtually no textual support for their position. What few texts cessationists are able to cite become the victim of eisegesis rather than exegesis. One argument assumes that charismatic gifts were given to endorse the apostles and ended when the last apostle died. Speaking of the argument for cessationism, Siegfried Schatzmann rightly comments:

> The first argument is generally not advanced on the basis of thorough exegesis, but receives its impetus from presuppositional and historical basis.[1]

A second argument is that the gifts ceased when the biblical canon was finally agreed upon. In support of this, 1 Corinthians 13:8–10 is cited:

> Love never fails. But whether there are prophecies, they will fail; whether there are tongues, they will cease; whether there is knowledge, it will vanish away. For we know in part and we prophesy in part. But when that which is perfect has come, then that which is in part will be done away.

The Scripture teaches that spiritual gifts, the charismata, are temporary. They will cease at the coming of "the perfect." "The perfect," according to this argument, is the completion of Scripture. Yet Archibald Robertson and Alfred Plummer in the *International Critical Commentary* declare that "the perfect" is a reference to the Second Advent:

> He does not say when we shall have come to perfection of the other world, etc…. He is so full of the promise of the Second Advent, that he represents the perfection coming to us. When it shall have come then and not until then. The Apostle is saying nothing about the cessation of the charismata in this life.[2]

When we look at the biblical revelation concerning charismatic gifts, it is consistent that these grace gifts are for the church until Christ's second coming. First Corinthians 1:4–9 says:

> I thank my God always concerning you for the grace of God which was given to you by Christ Jesus, that you were enriched in everything by Him in all utterance and all knowledge, even as the testimony of Christ was confirmed in you, so that you come short in no gift, eagerly waiting for the revelation of our Lord Jesus Christ, who will also confirm you to the end, that you may be blameless in the day of our Lord Jesus Christ. God is faithful, by whom you were called into the fellowship of His Son, Jesus Christ our Lord.

Paul considered charismatic gifts as enriching the church. The most telling verse is verse 7. Paul says:

> ...that you come short in no charismata [gift], eagerly waiting for the revelation [apocalypse] of our Lord Jesus Christ.

Clearly, the apostle believed that the charismatic gifts would be operating at the second coming of Jesus Christ. Furthermore, the absence of these spiritual graces leaves the church impoverished. Many Christians deny that the charismatic gifts described in the New Testament are valid today. The list in Romans 12:6–8 seems to be acceptable.

Also, it must be pointed out that Paul intended to bring a release of new spiritual gifts to Rome. Romans 1:11 states:

> For I long to see you, that I may impart to you some spiritual gift, so that you may be established.

Here Paul promises to impart *charisma pneumatikos.* The combination of these two words looks back to 1 Corinthians when Paul used them interchangeably in 1 Corinthians 12–14 in his discussion of the charismata.

There is virtually no biblical case for cessationism. For a thorough examination of all the texts and arguments, see Jon Mark Ruthven's *On the Cessation of the Charismata* and Siegfried Schatzmann's *A Pauline Theology of the Charismata.* Also, the writings of Wayne Grudem, Jack Deere, Michael Brown, and Wesley Campbell debunk cessationism as a biblical model. Even Ken Hemphill admits in his book *Mirror, Mirror on the Wall* that all the gifts are still operating.[3]

Elephants and Eight-Hundred-Pound Gorillas

Charismata and spiritual gifts in general are often spoken of in dismissive tones by opponents, but the elephant in the room is the gift of tongues. Here is the primary issue. Tongues in the New Testament were used miraculously to speak known languages,[4] to magnify God, as a sign of the presence of the Holy Spirit, as a prophetic word-releasing language to be interpreted, and a prayer language. While widely practiced in the early church, it was abused and misused. Paul sought to correct abuses without quenching the work of the Spirit. Widespread abuses today continue to bring this gift into disfavor. Except for the rare prophetic tongue that must be interpreted, Paul emphasized tongues' higher use as a private prayer language.

> He who speaks in a tongue edifies himself, but he who prophesies edifies the church.
> —1 Corinthians 14:4

In this usage of *charisma*, the Holy Spirit becomes a personal trainer building up the faith of the individual believer. A football player would be foolish to take his personal trainer from the weight room to the field with him. In fact, that would violate the rules of the game. Likewise, the prayer language is for the private spiritual training of the individual believer. As for the gift of tongues, we must remember that though Paul regulated it, he warned the early church in 1 Corinthians 14:39, "Do not forbid to speak with tongues."[5]

Historical Roots of Cessationism

In Christian history, the first thorough cessationist we encounter is Martin Luther. In reacting to the phony miracles of the Roman Catholic clergy and in protest to their selling indulgences, Luther reacted to the supernatural. Jon Mark Ruthven says of Luther:

> A precedent-setting example of Cessationism is Martin Luther, who saw the Charismatic emphases of the gospel and Acts and largely ignored them, omitting parts and responding by gerrymandering the New Testament to conform to the emphases of his theology and to deny New Testament authority to his opponents. Specifically, it is within the context of anti-charismatic polemics, against both the papacy and the radical reformation, that Luther developed his concept of a canon within the canon, that the doctrine and emphases of one group of books was subordinated to another group. According to his Preface to the New Testament of 1522, it is his sole criterion for selecting "the heart and core of all the books" is that these do not describe many works and miracles of Christ.[6]

I fear that as evangelicals we may often be unaware of our more enthusiastic roots. Somehow we want to be accepted by the religious establishment and intelligentsia. We don't want to talk about our past. In fact, we now want to be the religious establishment. We certainly don't want to be reminded of our emotionalism and revival fervor.

Somehow we have embraced a rewriting of the history of our spiritual roots. Some prefer to link ourselves to the Magisterial Reformers rather than to the zealous and persecuted Anabaptists. Some have a tendency to look down on what we call the fringe elements of Christianity without remembering that our roots lie within the context of dissent against state-established churches. Nevertheless, as we consider the workings of the Holy Spirit, it is important to observe how Christians through the ages understood and practiced spiritual gifts.

By looking back at history, we can see where we came from. By observing their practice of biblical truth, maybe we will learn where we should be going.

If one goes to the standard commentaries printed prior to the twentieth century, a clearly stated cessationist view is hard to find. However, one will find that the supernatural gifts and miraculous displays of God's power waned during the Middle Ages. Also, the basic doctrine of justification by faith was not embraced, much less the gifts, signs, and wonders brought on by the anointing of the Holy Spirit, except among some of the peripheral elements of Christianity. At the so-called conversion of Constantine, the church became a patron of the state and lost its vitality. Descending into a dark night of ritualism and clerical professionalism, the church lost its soul. During the Middle Ages, an itinerant preacher and scholar visited the Vatican. After his tour, the priest who guided him said, "No longer does the church have to say, 'Silver and gold have I none!'" The visitor replied, "Neither can you say, 'In the name of Jesus rise up and walk!'" The loss of power during the Middle Ages was as tragic as the loss of truth.

However, the Reformation brought a recovery of truth. The Reformation views of *sola fide* ("by faith alone") and *sola scriptura* ("Scripture alone") opened the door for a recovery of truth and of spiritual power. John Calvin and Martin Luther led the fight to return the church to the saving doctrines of the faith.

Even during that dark time some dissenting groups tried to maintain New Testament Christianity. The Church of Rome often viewed those groups as heretics. Baptists find their roots among those fringe groups. Baptist roots reach back beyond the Reformation and find their identity with the outsiders.

Some of the more prominent Baptist historians in the past, including Henry Vedder, generally agree that the people now called Baptists have been known by different names in different ages and countries. Vedder explains how the name Baptist was a contemptible title that was derived from the name given to our ancestors— the Anabaptists, or "rebaptizers." Adversaries gave them this name because they insisted on baptism by immersion and refused to maintain the practice of infant baptism or sprinkling.[7] Other Baptist historians tend to discredit this view of Baptist history because some of the leaders of those fringe movements became heretical. However, Vedder admits that the possibility of a connection could exist: "One cannot affirm that there was not a continuity in the outward visible life of the churches founded by the apostles down to the Reformation....A succession of the true faith may indeed be traced, in faint lines at times, but never entirely disappearing."[8]

In Thomas Armitage's *A History of the Baptists*, the title page displays the following introduction:

> A History of the Baptists traced by their vital principles from the time of our Lord and Savior Jesus Christ to the Year 1886.[9]

Other distinguished leaders in the last century, such as William Williams, once professor of church history at Southern Baptist Theological Seminary, and George Gould of England, author of a series of Baptist manuals, declared the New Testament origins of Baptist life.

Zwingli, the Swiss Reformer, firmly declared in his "Reply to Wall" that Anabaptists were no novelty, but claimed that they had for 1,300 years been causing great disturbance in the church. He made that statement in 1530, showing that he felt the movement dated to A.D. 230.

Zwingli also claimed that Baptists were part of the Waldensian movement. Peter Waldo was a Frenchman born in 1150 who hungered after God's Word. He hired someone to translate parts of the Latin Bible into the vernacular of the day, and as God's truth broke over his spirit, he had an intense desire to share it with everyone. He began preaching in the countryside, and the people were eager finally to hear God's Word in their language. Soon a number of lay preachers joined him who also spread the gospel through the land, bringing on the disapproval of the Roman church.

More than the breach of authority upset the Roman

Catholic Church. Waldo and his converts believed in salvation by grace through faith in Christ, without the decrees of the church. They also believed that baptism was for adults who made a confession of faith, and they discouraged infant baptism. They believed there was no such thing as purgatory. Looking back through history, we find that later Anabaptists were most prevalent in the area where the preachers of the Waldensians were ministering just one or two centuries before.[10] The Catholic church called these Baptist forebears heretics. Thousands of them were tortured and murdered.

Through the years, some have asserted that Baptists are a part of an unbroken chain of churches called by various names that have been the genuine practitioners of New Testament faith. For their own desire to be New Testament churches, loyal to the biblical faith, our forebears were banished, tortured, drowned, harassed, and mocked—all for a belief that New Testament practices remained valid in their day. The following is a brief description of some of these groups.

Montanism

Around the middle of the second century, Montanism appeared and flourished in the greater part of Asia Minor. Though some called it a heresy, W. A. Jarrell in his *Baptist Church Perpetuity*, published in 1904, declared the Montanists to be forebears of Baptists, thus tracing Baptist origins back to around A.D. 150. Jarrell argued, "Montanism enrolled its hosts and was one of the greatest

Christian influences throughout the early Christian centuries."[11] He stated further, "As there was at that time, when Montanism arose, no essential departure from the faith...the subjects of baptism, church government, or doctrine, the Montanists on these points were Baptists."[12] Though Montanus was accused of claiming to be the Comforter, he simply believed that a man could be filled and directed by the Holy Spirit.

Tertullian, perhaps the greatest preacher of the third century, embraced Montanism's doctrines, and his remarkable ministry gave evidence of the power of God. Tertullian refuted most of the attacks on Montanus, exposing those attacks as lies. The Montanists were millennialists, believing in the literal End Time, one-thousand-year reign of Christ on earth, holding to a literal interpretation of Scripture. They had women teachers among them, and some may have practiced triune immersion. Tertullian believed that the Holy Spirit was the restorer of the apostolic model.[13] William Moeller, a noted church historian, commented on Tertullian:

> To him the very substance of the church was the Holy Spirit not the Episcopacy [rule by bishops]...Thus, in church government they were Baptists.[14]

Neander, another historian from the nineteenth century, wrote, "Montanism set up a church of the Spirit...like Protestantism, [Montanism] places the Holy

Spirit first, and considers the church as that which is only derived.... The gifts of the Spirit were to be dispersed to Christians of every condition and sex without distinction...to give prominence once more to the idea of the dignity of the universal Christian calling, of the priestly dignity of all Christians."[15]

Montanists experienced ecstatic worship, visions, prophecies, and the exercise of all the gifts of the Spirit. One young convert of Montanus described this ecstasy by saying, "On the wings of a dove I was carried above." Jarrell quoted Thomas Armitage, who explained a key factor connecting Baptists with the Montanist beliefs:

> The one prime idea held by Montanists in common with Baptists, and in distinction to the churches of the third century was, that the membership of the churches should be confined to purely regenerate person; and that a spiritual life and disciplined life should be maintained without any affiliation with the authority of the State. Exterior church organization and the efficacy of the ordinances did not meet their idea of Gospel church existence without the indwelling Spirit of Christ; not in the bishops alone, but in all Christians. For this reason Montanus was charged with assuming to be the Holy Spirit, which was simply a slander.[16]

William R. Williams in his Lectures on Baptist History said of the Montanists:

> It was hard to find any doctrinal errors in their
> views; that they were rather like Methodists and
> Jansenists in their high views of religious emotion
> and experience. They were accused of claiming
> inspiration when they intended...the true experi-
> ence of God's work in the individual soul....They
> insisted much upon the power of the Spirit as the
> great conservator and guardian of the life of the
> Christian church.[17]

Montanism was a reaction of Spirit-filled people to a
church structure that moved in fleshly power and human
manipulation rather than the power of the Holy Spirit.

Jarrell concluded his arguments in his book by
expressing his belief that the Montanists clearly were the
original "apostolic" church. Citing Moeller, Jarrell sought
to prove the Montanists to be the primitive church:

> But Montanism was, nevertheless, not a new
> form of Christianity; nor were the Montaists a
> new sect. On the contrary, Monatism was simply
> a reaction of the old, the primitive church, against
> the obvious tendency of the day, to strike a bar-
> gain with the world and arrange herself comfort-
> ably in it.[18]

The Montanists refuted the idea that the miracles and
gifts ceased in the first century. It seems strange that most
Baptist historians prior to our present century acknowledge the Montanists as a part of the Baptist and other

evangelical heritage, while our current historians tend to deny that connection. Could it be that these latter historians are viewing both Scripture and history through the lenses of routine and tradition securely in place? By denying the supernatural work of God today through some spiritual gifts and the powerful manifestations of the Spirit, some Baptists resist being identified with the fiery heroes of the past. Apparently many Baptist leaders are more comfortable with the Reformers who actually persecuted our Anabaptist forebears.

Anabaptists

Balthaser Hübmaier was one of those who suffered for his faith. Born in Bavaria in 1482, he grew up to become a wise and respected scholar. He chose theology for his lifework, and upon completing his basic studies, he became vice rector at Ingolstadt and later pastored a cathedral. He was known for his pure and holy life, and a brilliant career was before him. However, the career was less attractive to him as he realized that truth was not being upheld in many of his religious circles. In 1522 he cast his lot with the Reformers, particularly Zwingli, feeling that they were truly pursuing God's truth. One of the points of conflict in that day was the doctrine of infant baptism, and although some of the Reformers at first agreed that it needed to be done away with, when Hübmaier acted upon it in his Austrian church, the other Reformers—including Zwingli—withdrew from him.

He was sent a summons to appear and answer for his bold actions, but he ignored it and soon published a work entitled *Heretics and Those Who Burn Them.* He took additional bold steps, such as abolishing the practice of Mass in the church and putting aside the priestly vestments. He encouraged his flock to know the Scriptures in their own language, to practice water baptism in the biblical way, and to know the power of the Holy Spirit on their lives.

He tried to flee to Zurich, but he was seized and imprisoned. In 1528, after being tried for heresy by the Catholic Church, he was burned at the stake in the public square. His faithful wife, who supported and exhorted him to proclaim Bible truth, was drowned soon after, another martyr for Christ.[19]

Could it be that Baptists and other evangelicals who believe in the gifts and manifestations of the Spirit are more true to Scripture in their beliefs than some of those who are more comfortable with the formality of the Reformation? Although Hübmaier cannot be said to be Pentecostal, the exclusionary tendencies in the Reformation leadership of those who embraced all of Scripture set a pattern that Baptists appear to be following today. Pentecostal denominations are less than one hundred years old and sprang out of the mainline denominations, including Southern Baptists, according to Dr. Steven Jack Land, president of the Pentecostal Theological Seminary in Cleveland, Tennessee. Some of the founders of the Church of God were former Baptists.

Neither time nor space permits a thorough study of other

groups in church history such as the Novatians, Donatists, Paulicians, Albigenses, Patarenses, Petrobrusians, and Arnoldists. These are just a few of the groups who believed in New Testament power in the life of the church.[20]

Our Anabaptist forebears were maligned for many reasons. First, they stood on the Scriptures alone as a standard for faith and practice. Second, they practiced baptism by immersion. Third, some believed in the mysteries of a personal union with Christ, dreams, visions, and supernatural gifting. Last, they supported total separation of the church from the state. One will search in vain in Baptist history for a cessationist view of charismatic spiritual gifts. Granted, one may find an admission among a few of the Puritan Baptists that the gifts had waned. The spiritual deadness and coldness of their churches, however, could simply explain this.

Baptists of Ardor and Order

Churches should find their roots deep in the apostolic teaching of the New Testament and not in any man-made system. Even in American history, records show Baptists or people of similar principles were persecuted. Roger Williams was excommunicated by the Church of England in 1636 and fled for his life through the wild snows of New England. He established what many believe to be the First Baptist Church in America in Providence, Rhode Island. Baptists in America were beaten, banished, killed, and imprisoned for the free churches they sought to establish. Yet the Baptists of New England and Virginia helped to secure religious freedom for America. In fact, Europeans denounced the Declaration of Independence as "an Anabaptist document."[21] Baptists have a long history of being persecuted or criticized for convictions they considered biblical by the majority who held them in contempt, whether issues related to baptism, religious liberty, or emotional revivalism. Today the issue appears to be speaking in tongues.

Looking at the practices of Baptists in worship and revival across the years, we find much that disturbs our present complacency. There is in our history all of the accompaniment of awakening and revival, including loud worship, trembling, untranslatable utterings, wild cries, falling out, and other things that seem embarrassing in today's church. Historically, Baptists stood for a New Testament faith. This faith gave spiritual freedom to the individual Christian and to the local church where he worshiped.

When we look forward from the New Testament and see our roots in the Montanists, the Waldenses, the Rennanites, and the Lollards, among others, we find a continuation not only of baptism by immersion but also of the power of God. John Broadus made the following statement in a speech to the American Baptist Convention. This passage gives a clear account of some of our Southern Baptist roots. Although not about the exercising of charismatic gifts, it underscores the revivalistic heritage of

Baptists. Revivalism was the wellspring from which the reactivation of the gifts emerged.[22]

> Shubael Stearns was born in Boston in 1706, and under the influence of the Great Awakening, attached himself, in 1745, to the Congregationalist Separates, or New Lights and began to preach. In 1751 he became a Baptist, in Connecticut, and after two or three years more, longing to carry the gospel to more destitute regions, he came, with a small colony of brethren, to Berkeley County, Va. Here he was joined by Daniel Marshall, who was of the same age with him and had also been a Congregationalist and a Separate in Connecticut. Believing that the second coming of Christ was certainly at hand, Marshall and others sold or abandoned their property, and hastening with destitute families to the head-waters of the Susquehanna, began to labor for the conversion of the Mohawk Indians.
>
> After eighteen months he was driven away by an Indian war, and went to Berkeley Co., Va., where, finding a Baptist church, he examined and adopted their views in about 1754. He had married, while in Connecticut, the sister of Shubael Stearns. The two became associated in Virginia and soon sought together a still more destitute region in North Carolina, not far from Greensboro. Here they and their little colony taught the necessity of the new birth and the consciousness of conversion,

with all the excited manner and holy wine and the nervous trembling and wild screams among their hearers, which characterized the Congregationalist Separates in Connecticut. Though at first much ridiculed, they soon had great success, building up two churches of five hundred and six hundred members.

Retaining their New England name of Separates, they called themselves "Separate Baptists," and these spread rapidly into Virginia and into Georgia, though destined, when their enthusiastic excesses should have been cooled down, to be absorbed, before the end of the eighteenth century, into the body of regular Baptists.

Stearns died in North Carolina; but [Daniel] Marshall, ever looking out for new fields, came, after a few years, to Lexington District, in South Carolina, where he built up a church, and finally, three years before the time of which we speak, removed to Georgia, not far from Augusta, where he had already formed a considerable church. Among the unusual customs of the Separates, both Congregationalist and Baptist, was the practice of public prayer and exhortation by women; and in these exercise Marshall's wife is said to have been wonderfully impressive.[23]

Our roots lie not in the cathedrals of Europe nor in the hallowed halls of academia, but in the Upper Room and later in "the brush arbor." We were birthed and borne along in the fire of Pentecost and revival. We cannot continue to shake the hayseed of our "brush arbor" origin out of our hair and pretend that we are a part of some ecclesiastical hierarchy that came out of the Roman Catholic Church! The ecstasies of all these early movements and the noises were similar to and would be labeled charismatic today and could have included tongues. We cannot prove this either way; the point is that churches operated in a freedom not allowed today.

In the Delivery Room

At the early part of this century, a revival called Azusa Street broke out in Los Angeles. The great movement of Pentecostalism was birthed from that meeting. However, that wasn't the only movement. In reaction to the Azusa Street outbreak, Baptists identified with the Calvinist scholar B. B. Warfield, who wrote the first detailed argument that the gifts of the Spirit had ceased. Warfield wrote specifically to criticize the revival where the supernatural had broken forth. In addition, dispensational theology came into prominence—a doctrine that compartmentalizes Scripture and contends that the age of miracles is over.

Yet many Baptists do not know that the Pentecostal revival that broke out in Los Angeles in the early part of this century actually started in First Baptist Church of Los Angeles, California. The pastor, Joseph Smale, returned from a meeting with the leader of the Welsh revival, Evan Roberts. While in Wales, Smale prayed for the same fire to fall upon his church in Los Angeles. Day after day and night after night people waited before the Lord at that Baptist church. Revival broke out with all the manifestations and freedom witnessed across the years in awakening. Denominational walls fell, and people gathered from all across the city to experience the Lord's outpouring. A Baptist church had become the center for revival. Pastor Smale prophesied a return of apostolic gifts to the church.

That was in June of 1905. The revival swept the city and articles were written in major newspapers about the awakening. What happened to that meeting, and why did God have to move to Azusa Street in 1906? Frank Bartleman gave his eyewitness testimony:

> I went to Smale's church one night, and he resigned. The meetings had run daily in the First Baptist Church for fifteen weeks. It was now September. The officials of the church were tired of the innovation and wanted to return to the old order. He was told to either stop the revival or get out. He wisely chose the latter. But what an awful position for a church to take—to throw God out. In this same way, they later drove the Spirit of God out of the church in Wales. They tired of His presence, desiring to return to the old, cold ecclesiastical order. How blind men are! The most spiritual of Pastor Smale's members naturally followed him,

> with a nucleus of other workers who had gath-
> ered to him from other sources during the revival.
> They immediately contemplated organizing a New
> Testament church.[24]

Joseph Smale founded another work that thrived as a New Testament church. In that church God did a wonderful, mighty work.

Today hundreds of evangelical churches are moving in the power of the Spirit, and awakenings are happening in every region. Yet reactionary forces rise to quench the fire of the Holy Spirit. Those affected by the work of God's Spirit are often feared and unwelcome. Churches should have the freedom to operate in the Spirit within the biblical parameters. Is the Baptist (and evangelical?) tent big enough to include those who believe in the continuation and practice of the supernatural gifts of the Holy Spirit? I pray so.

One must also point to B. B. Warfield, Scofield, and John MacArthur as foundational teachers of cessationism. Evangelical opponents of cessationism include James Leo Garrett, Jack MacGorman, Siegfried Schatzmann, Ken Hemphill, Billy Graham, and a host of others.

If the Gifts Have Ceased . . .

What may be the implications of cessationism for the mainline church?

1. Churches might possibly lose millions of wonderfully gifted Christians who may begin to embrace charismatic practice.

2. Cessationism, by its denial of the present work of the Spirit, ignores or explains away the biblical content that clearly supports it.

3. Cessationism has implicit prejudicial overtones because many ethnic churches practice the gifts and operate in what is called charismatic worship.

4. Cessationism has enormous implications for the future of worldwide missions. In dealing with these cultures, missionaries need a full spiritual arsenal. The largest evangelistic movements on the Pacific Rim, in Africa, and in Central and South America are charismatic.[25]

5. Cessationism cuts off fellowship with other denominations that embrace inerrancy yet believe that all the gifts continue.

6. Cessationism limits the power of God among His people by shutting the door to certain manifestations of the Spirit's power.

7. Cessationism has a chilling effect on the next generation, creating a more intellectualized and pragmatic faith rather than Holy Spirit–empowered faith.

CHAPTER FOUR
The Need for
Spiritual Gifts

BEFORE WE EXPLORE the gifts of the Spirit, it is important that we understand their absolute necessity in the church. In the previous chapter we affirmed that the gifts have not ceased and are still operating in all their fullness today. With that understood, we must also press home the utter bankruptcy of the church without these gifts.

When we study the word *charismatic*, we discover that its root word is *grace*. God who saves by grace lived by grace. Grace is God's favor bestowed on believers without merit on their part. To ignore the gifts is to insult the Giver of all good things:

> Do not be deceived, my beloved brethren. Every good gift and every perfect gift is from above, and comes down from the Father of lights, with whom there is no variation or shadow of turning.
>
> —JAMES 1:16–17

How dare we refuse to open the gifts of the Spirit and operate in their power? Only an appalling arrogance would refuse the gifts Jesus has poured out on His blood-bought church.

David Ireland in his excellent book *Activating the Gifts of the Holy Spirit* gives an excellent summary of why people do not operate in the gifts. This summary is as follows:

> Fear of the supernatural, social acceptance, the carnal mind, the desire for control, and the lack of discernment.[1]

I would sum this up by saying that there is an embarrassment in the mind of the evangelical world over the Pentecostal gifts! Of course, there have been those who abused and perverted the gifts. Also, Satan has high counterfeits. Just remember, it is utterly stupid to counterfeit anything unless it is valuable.

Why Do We Need the Gifts?

First, we need the gifts of the Spirit to bring the supernatural dimension into today's church.

> And my speech and my preaching were not with persuasive words of human wisdom, but in demonstration of the Spirit and of power, that your faith should not be in the wisdom of men but in the power of God.
>
> —1 CORINTHIANS 2:4–5

What is going on in the average church that cannot be explained by human operation, invention, or promotion? Is our faith established by the power of God?

Second, the Holy Spirit's gifts bring a supernatural wisdom, revelation, and knowledge otherwise unknown to the believer in a church.

> [As] it is written: "Eye has not seen, nor ear heard, nor have entered into the heart of man the things which God has prepared for those who love Him." But God has revealed them to us through His Spirit. For the Spirit searches all things, yes, the deep things of God. For what man knows the things of a man except the spirit of the man which is in him? Even so no one knows the things of God except the Spirit of God. Now we have received, not the spirit of the world, but the Spirit who is from God, that we might know the things that have been freely given to us by God.
>
> These things we also speak, not in words which man's wisdom teaches but which the Holy Spirit teaches, comparing spiritual things with spiritual. But the natural man does not receive the things of the Spirit of God, for they are foolishness to him; nor can he know them, because they are spiritually discerned.
>
> —1 Corinthians 2:9–14

Third, spiritual gifts require a complete surrender to the will of God. Before Paul speaks of the gifts to the Roman church, he calls them to a crucified, surrendered life.

> I beseech you therefore, brethren, by the mercies of God, that you present your bodies a living sacrifice, holy, acceptable to God, which is your reasonable service. And do not be conformed to this world, but be transformed by the renewing of your mind, that you may prove what is that good and acceptable and perfect will of God.
>
> —ROMANS 12:1–2

Fourth, spiritual gifts bring a special unity and equality to the church.

> For I say, through the grace given to me, to everyone who is among you, not to think of himself more highly than he ought to think, but to think soberly, as God has dealt to each one a measure of faith. For as we have many members in one body, but all the members do not have the same function...
>
> —ROMANS 12:3–4

Gifts bring a powerful connection between believers that produces respect and honor among all.

Fifth, the gifts of the Spirit deepen the love and care believers have for one another in the church.

> So we, being many, are one body in Christ, and
> individually members of one another.
>
> —ROMANS 12:5

Sixth, the gifts of the Spirit give every believer useful-
ness and purpose in the church.

> But the manifestation of the Spirit is given to each
> one for the profit of all:...
>
> For by one Spirit we were all baptized into one
> body—whether Jews or Greeks, whether slaves or
> free—and have all been made to drink into one
> Spirit. For in fact the body is not one member but
> many. If the foot should say, "Because I am not a
> hand, I am not of the body," is it therefore not of
> the body? And if the ear should say, "Because I am
> not an eye, I am not of the body," is it therefore not
> of the body? If the whole body were an eye, where
> would be the hearing? If the whole were hearing,
> where would be the smelling? But now God has set
> the members, each one of them, in the body just
> as He pleased. And if they were all one member,
> where would the body be? But now indeed there
> are many members, yet one body. And the eye
> cannot say to the hand, "I have no need of you";
> nor again the head to the feet, "I have no need of
> you." No, much rather, those members of the body
> which seem to be weaker are necessary.
>
> —1 CORINTHIANS 12:7; 12:13–22

Seventh, the gifts of the Spirit confirm the witness and mission of the church.

> And [Jesus] said to them, "Go into all the world and preach the gospel to every creature. He who believes and is baptized will be saved; but he who does not believe will be condemned. And these signs will follow those who believe: In My name they will cast out demons; they will speak with new tongues; they will take up serpents; and if they drink anything deadly, it will by no means hurt them; they will lay hands on the sick, and they will recover." So then, after the Lord had spoken to them, He was received up into heaven, and sat down at the right hand of God. And they went out and preached everywhere, the Lord working with them and confirming the word through the accompanying signs. Amen.
>
> —MARK 16:15–20

Eighth, the gifts of the Spirit are God's trust given to the church. We therefore are to be good managers and stewards of the gifts.

> As each one has received a gift, minister it to one another, as good stewards of the manifold grace of God. If anyone speaks, let him speak as the oracles of God. If anyone ministers, let him do it as with the ability which God supplies, that in all things God may be glorified through Jesus Christ, to

> whom belong the glory and the dominion forever
> and ever. Amen.
>
> —1 PETER 4:10–11

Ninth, the gifts of the Spirit are to equip believers for both spiritual and numerical growth in the church.

> And He Himself gave some to be apostles, some
> prophets, some evangelists, and some pastors and
> teachers, for the equipping of the saints for the
> work of ministry, for the edifying of the body of
> Christ, till we all come to the unity of the faith and
> of the knowledge of the Son of God, to a perfect
> man, to the measure of the stature of the fullness
> of Christ…
>
> —EPHESIANS 4:11–13

This equipping brings unity and maturity, which lead to healthier relationships that are vital in the church. As the great poet John Donne once wrote, "No man is an island," and this is very true for the church. To fulfill the individual calling God has placed on each of our lives, and, more importantly, to fulfill our role in the Great Commission, we need the power of unity in the Holy Spirit. These connections release power and resources for growth.

> But, speaking the truth in love, may grow up in all
> things into Him who is the head—Christ—from
> whom the whole body, joined and knit together by

> what every joint supplies, according to the effective
> working by which every part does its share, causes
> growth of the body for the edifying of itself in love.
> —EPHESIANS 4:15–16

These are just some of the important reasons the church must have a fresh release of the gifts of the Spirit.

I challenge every believer to a fresh pursuit and openness to God's love gifts.

CHAPTER FIVE
The Five Leadership Gifts of the Spirit

L EADERSHIP, SOME SAY, is a learned skill. Certainly there are many skills needed to successfully lead in the corporate world as your company's success, the profit to your shareholders, and the welfare of your employees are all at stake; but ultimately, these are all passing things that will one day slip into decay. It is a portentous thing to consider leading in a situation where a person's eternal soul is at stake. Every believer is a member of Christ's royal priesthood and is consequently called to fulfill the Great Commission, but, as we have stated in the previous chapters, not all have the same role. Read Ephesians 4:11–16:

> And He Himself gave some to be apostles, some prophets, some evangelists, and some pastors and teachers, for the equipping of the saints for the work of ministry, for the edifying of the body of Christ, till we all come to the unity of the faith and of the knowledge of the Son of God, to a perfect man, to the measure of the stature of the fullness of Christ; that we should no longer be children, tossed to and fro and carried about with every wind of doctrine, by the trickery of men, in

the cunning craftiness of deceitful plotting, but, speaking the truth in love, may grow up in all things into Him who is the head—Christ—from whom the whole body, joined and knit together by what every joint supplies, according to the effective working by which every part does its share, causes growth of the body for the edifying of itself in love.

Here in Ephesians 4 we find the gifts of the Spirit as gifted persons. The first sixteen verses of Ephesians 4 set both the unity of the Spirit and the gifts of the Spirit.

Note that no church is ready for the full ministry of God's gifts until there is a bond of unity and love (Eph. 4:1–6). Remember our plea in the last study that we accept one another's differences in gifting and unite behind our mission to reach our community, touch our denomination, stir our nation, and penetrate our world with the gospel.

Weddings and anniversary celebrations aside, 1 Corinthians 13 warns us that we are not ready to enjoy the gifts until we are baptized with agape love. Before Paul raises the subject of gifts, he calls the church to unity.

The Gifts to the Church

But to each one of us grace was given according to the measure of Christ's gift.

—Ephesians 4:7

Paul wrote these sixteen words and packed them with so much truth that they must be more closely scrutinized.

Notice the following truths about spiritual gifts. First, there are gifts of the Spirit for us all. That wonderful phrase "to each one of us" means that there are none of us, no, not one, for whom God is not willing to empower and enable with supernatural gifting from on high.

Secondly, the depth of your gifting is in proportion to the depth of your relationship with Jesus. You may have the gift of teaching, for example, but you will never be empowered to bring a deep, revelatory *rhema* word to those you seek to teach unless you are seeking a deep, revelatory *rhema* relationship with Jesus.

> "When [Jesus] ascended on high, He led captivity captive, and gave gifts to men." (Now this, "He ascended"—what does it mean but that He also first descended into the lower parts of the earth? He who descended is also the One who ascended far above all the heavens, that He might fill all things.)
>
> —Ephesians 4:8–10

Time and space do not permit an exhaustive look at the wondrous things that Jesus accomplished via His death and resurrection, nor do we have time or space to study in an in-depth way the miracles associated with the Ascension, but it is important to note that Jesus did three powerful things at His ascension.

1. He liberated the Old Testament saints.

2. He took them to heaven.

3. He poured out the gifts of the Spirit on the church.

These are important because in doing these things, Jesus cites by action yet another in the long list of evidences that prove He is a promise-keeping God.

The Gifts in the Church (Verse 11)

> And He Himself gave some to be apostles, some prophets, some evangelists, and some pastors and teachers...

Notice carefully that these gifts in Ephesians 4 are *domata* not *charismata*. Back in verse 7 we are all given *charis* or grace gifts. These gifts in Ephesians 4 are the offices of the church. They are people uniquely gifted by God to the church. These gifts explain to us the fivefold ministry that should be taking place in the church!

Apostle

The word is found eighty-one times and is translated "apostle" seventy-eight times, "messenger" two times, and "he that is sent" one time. At least twenty-four different people in the New Testament are given that designation! The idea that the Twelve were the only ones with apostolic ministry is wrong. Now uniquely the Twelve gave us the Scripture and were eye witnesses of the Lord.

An apostle is a delegate sent with the full power and authority of the one sending him. The apostolic ministry is the supernatural work of Christ to the church. Signs of miracles followed the ministry of the apostles.

Prophets

Though all believers may give prophetic words from Scripture and give counsel and insight to others, not all are prophets.

Prophets are sent to give edification, correction, and direction to the church. They come to the church with the *now* word—with what Peter calls "present truth."

Evangelist

The evangelist is one whose passion is reaching the unsaved and who can also equip others to reach the lost. This is a special calling and office, though it is, at the same time, true that all believers are called to reach the lost.

Pastor

The pastor is one who is a shepherd to lead, feed, and care for the people of God. He is here to equip others with this gift to minister to the body, and, more often than not, a particular *local* body.

Teacher

One called to be a teacher is sent and gifted to unfold the Word of God to the church. Of all these *domata*, the office of teacher is the one most associated with the warning found in James 3:1:

> My brethren, let not many of you become teachers, knowing that we shall receive a stricter judgment.

To fulfill its purpose to the body, a local church—and the church universal—must offer this fivefold ministry. To not do so, or, worse, to deny its existence and validity today, is to not simply shortchange the congregation, but to exalt the desires, doctrines, and traditions of men above the clear instruction of God.

The Gifts Released in the Church (Verses 12–16)

> For the equipping of the saints for the work of ministry, for the edifying of the body of Christ, till we all come to the unity of the faith and of the knowledge of the Son of God, to a perfect man, to the measure of the stature of the fullness of Christ; that we should no longer be children, tossed to and fro and carried about with every wind of doctrine, by the trickery of men, in the cunning craftiness of deceitful plotting, but, speaking the truth in love, may grow up in all things into Him who is the head—Christ—from whom the whole body, joined and knit together by what every joint supplies, according to the effective working by which

> every part does its share, causes growth of the body
> for the edifying of itself in love.

Space will only permit me to list the blessings that are released in the church when gifts are properly exercised.

1. They equip the people for ministry (v. 12).

2. They build up the church (v. 12).

3. They unify the church around knowing Christ (v. 13).

4. They bring us to maturity (v. 13).

5. They bring us to fullness (v. 13).

6. They keep us from error (vv. 14–15).

7. They help us to grow (v. 15).

8. They release a supply of all the church needs (v. 16).

9. They cause the church to increase its ministry (v. 16).

The only conclusion from an honest study of these scriptures is that truly gifted leaders are *indispensable* to the church.

CHAPTER SIX

The Seven Service Gifts
of the Holy Spirit

In Genesis 24 Abraham sent his servant from Canaan to Padan Aram to find a bride for his son Isaac. The faithful servant loaded ten camels to take with him. How much wealth can be loaded on a camel? These camels carried evidence that Abraham was wealthy. Among the gifts were precious jewelry, garments, and treasures. When the servant found Rebekah, Isaac's bride, his first task was to give her a costly nose jewel and bracelets. By accepting the gifts, Rebekah agreed to become Isaac's bride.

Similarly, God has sent His Holy Spirit to us, the bride of Christ, with abundant gifts. Salvation is a gift. Jesus Himself is a gift from the Father. The presence and power of the Holy Spirit is a gift. Everything we have is a gift from God. Our spiritual gifts are divine talents given at the new birth to enable us to know, to do, and to speak with His authority.

Look to Romans 12:6–8:

> We have different gifts, according to the grace given us. If a man's gift is prophesying, let him use it in proportion to his faith. If it is serving, let him

serve; if it is teaching, let him teach; if it is encouraging, let him encourage; if it is contributing to the needs of others, let him give generously; if it is leadership, let him govern diligently; if it is showing mercy, let him do it cheerfully.

—NIV

Every Christian has at least one of these motivational gifts. When we are born physically, we have natural talents. They same is true when we are born again (spiritually); we receive certain spiritual talents. Joy comes to our lives when we exercise our gifts. These are charisma gifts. The root *char* means "joy," and *charis* is the root word for *grace*, which means "God gives the desire and the power to do His will through our gifting." We find great personal fulfillment in developing our gifts. Each gift strengthens the body of Christ. Love is the reason for all the gifts to operate. This must be very important to God, for there are approximately one hundred verses on spiritual gifts in the New Testament. I can think of no better example of spiritual gifts than the one given by Bill Gothard. This will help you find your spiritual gift.

Suppose a group of people were going through the line at Piccadilly cafeteria to eat a meal together and someone dropped their tray, spilling food and drink all over the floor and themselves. How would other people react?

1. Prophecy would respond, "That is what happens when you're not paying attention. You weren't watching where you were going."

2. Mercy would say, "Don't feel bad. It could have happened to anyone."

3. The serving gift would reply, "Oh, let me help you clean it up." This person wants to fulfill a practical need.

4. The teacher would say, "The reason that fell is that it had too many objects on one side and the tray wasn't balanced." The teacher wants to discover why it happened.

5. The exhorter would offer, "Next time let's put fewer dishes on the tray," as her motivation is to correct for the future.

6. The giver would say, "I'll be happy to buy you another tray of food." His motivation is to give to a tangible need.

7. The administrator would take control and say, "Jim, would you get a mop, and Sue, please get a wet cloth to clean the stains on her clothes, and Mary, would you gather the dishes and tray and take them to the kitchen?" This person's motivation is to achieve the immediate goal of the group.

Which one are you? Your motivation is always a desire to reach out and help others. Your gift is not for you but to benefit others in love.

The Gift of Prophecy Corrects the Church

Someone who says, "Thus says the Lord," and speaks with divine authority based on Scripture is a prophet. The Greek word *prophetes* means "to declare, proclaim, and make known." The prophet has a strong sense of right and wrong and reacts harshly to unrighteousness, wickedness, evil, and sin. Prophets love justice and are painfully direct with people. They will suffer for what is right and bear their own personal struggles and faults to help others. Peter is the biblical example. He was always talking, had strong opinions, and was very persuasive. Prophets speak the truth at all costs.

The Gift of Serving Helps the Church

When we think of Christians who serve behind the scenes, we think of those with the gift also called "helps." They want to bless others to serve the Lord more effectively. They are motivated by a strong sense of need and feel like "someone has to do it." They often find themselves doing what others don't want to do. They are flexible, adapt to change, and rise to a challenge. They truly are selfless and disregard their family needs or their own fatigue or health to help others. Sometimes they have trouble saying no, take on too much, and get frustrated. They love appreciation and to be thanked. They love short-term projects and often feel inadequate or unqualified for leadership. One caution to those who identify with this gift: enjoy serving, but don't be a martyr.

Timothy is a biblical example of the gift of serving in action. Paul said no one cared for his state like Timothy. He brought a cloak and books to Paul in Rome and was always working with others. Paul encouraged him that he was qualified by his ordination and the training of his mother and grandmother.

The Gift of Teaching Instructs the Church

Christians with this gift prefer to explain why things are true. If prophets declare truth, then teachers explain the reason why it is true. Teachers love research and to dig up insignificant facts. They enjoy presenting what they have discovered. They love study, seek a deeper understanding, and neglect other needs. Sometimes they miss the obvious. They dig too deep and try to exhaust a subject rather than just reveal it. It is hard for a teacher to say "I was wrong" or admit they came to a wrong conclusion.

I have this gift, as do Beth Moore and Perry Stone. Luke in the New Testament had this gift. His purpose in writing was that they "might know the certainty of those things, wherein you have been instructed" (Luke 1:4, AKJV). He explained in detail as an eyewitness of Christ. He used a detailed chronological approach. Luke is the longest Gospel with precise descriptions and more details than any other gospel. A teacher will remain silent until information has been heard, observed, and verified before accepting it.

The Gift of Exhortation Encourages the Church

Martin Luther said that "teaching and exhortation differ from each other in…that teaching is directed to the ones who do not know, but exhortation to those who do know."[1] The gift of exhortation brings a word of hope to raise us above the problems. The Greek word for *exhortation* is *paraklesis*, which, like the Holy Spirit Himself, means "to exhort, comfort, to call near or alongside for help." The Holy Spirit is called the Comforter, one who is called alongside to give hope to our soul. These gifted people have the right words at just the right time to lift us up. You always feel better about yourself after listening to an encourager. They always include steps of action that show hope.

Pastor Joel Osteen, Joyce Meyer, and Pastor Ronnie Phillips Jr. all have this gift. Paul is the biblical example of an encourager.

The Gift of Giving Supplies the Church

The gift of giving is actually the gift of getting. This one has resources at his fingertips to supply the physical needs of believers while the encourager meets the spiritual and emotional needs of believers. The Greek word is *metadidomi*, which means "to impart, share, and give." Barnabas exercised this gift when he sold his land to give to the church. Giving is a part of worship, but it is not limited to the wealthy, although that is common.

We cannot excuse ourselves from this gift just because we aren't wealthy, for we are told that we exercise *all* the gifts when given the opportunity. Giving is more than money. It can be food, clothes, shelter, and benefits. It is not time, because all gifts require that. Givers must offer to others without expecting anything in return. Givers do not like attention or recognition, but their gifts are always high quality. They practice personal frugality and are happy with just the basics of life. Sometimes gifts are misinterpreted as pressure or a desire to control. This is not true. Givers are sensitive to how money is spent and saved and don't give to the obvious needs but make good financial board members and are conscientious.

The biblical example of giving was Matthew, who had wealth and wealthy friends but gave it all to follow Christ.

The Gift of Administration Organizes the Church

This gift has to do with overseeing something. The Greek here is *proistemi*, which means "to set over or to rule." Leaders are needed to organize particular ministries or groups, but they should do so with a heart of caring and compassion. We first think of ruling as a tyrant or dominating leader. This should not be true of how this gift serves the church.

Leaders lead with humility and a servant heart. This also involves the Greek word in 1 Corinthians 12:28 as *kubernesis*, which means "direction" or "guidance." This person directs the church and sees that things are in good order and go well. People with this gift organize a church ministry or event, plan and begin a new ministry, organize a new class, or plan gatherings for family, school, or neighborhood. These people have a strong sense of duty and are good at delegating responsibility. A strong focus of participation and teamwork exists. They see the big picture and know how to reach the goal. They are very good at keeping people together and for getting ahead.

A caution here to those who identify with this gift: lead by example and not manipulation or guilt. Try not to appear callous for a desire to accomplish a project rather than to love and care for people. If no one is leading, then the one with this gift steps up. Don't think that the ability to delegate means this leader avoids work. That simply is not true.

Probably all leaders of ministries either have or exercise this gift. Contemporaries who have this gift are Marcus Lamb and Paul Crouch, who have built giant television networks. Nehemiah is the biblical example who rebuilt the walls of Jerusalem with many groups each working on a small section. He overcame many obstacles to finish the job while challenging and motivating the workers to the goal.

The Gift of Mercy Comforts the Church

The gift of mercy is the divine enablement to cheerfully and practically help those who are suffering or are in need. This is compassion moved to action. People with this gift focus on alleviating the sources of pain or discomfort in suffering people, address the needs of the lonely and forgotten, while expressing love, grace, and dignity to those facing hardship and crisis. They serve in difficult or unsightly circumstances and do so cheerfully. They are concerned with individuals and social issues that oppress people. They do attract people with severe mental or emotional needs. They measure acceptance by physical closeness and quality time together. They want to remove hurts without looking for benefits from the hurts. They tend to avoid firmness or decisions. Sometimes they take up the offense of the hurt person and get in the middle of something they cannot change. Because they are so sensitive, they often get improper affection from the opposite sex. They tend to cut off others who are insensitive. They sympathize with those who violate God's standards and do not discern why people suffer. Their friendships can be possessive.

Contemporary examples of this gift are Franklin Graham with Samaritan's Purse ministry and Mother Teresa, who gave her life to the slums of India. The apostle John had this gift as he focused on relationships and wrote to give joy, hope, and confidence to cast out fear. He accepted others and was the disciple whom Jesus loved.

Find your gift. Pursue your gift. Ask God for opportunities to use His gift to you. Let love motivate you to use your gift to bless others, and when you get to heaven, God will say, "Well done, thou good and faithful servant."

CHAPTER SEVEN
Eight Sign Gifts
of the Spirit

MANY SCHOLARS DECLAIM the English language as guttural and inaccurate, while praising the languages of scriptural texts (that is, Greek and Hebrew) and even existing languages of the time as superior. I don't necessarily hold to this view, but it is important to note that the English word *gift* as translated in the Bible, especially in the New Testament, is one among many words that don't quite fit the original intent of the writers of Scripture. Notice some special words that help us understand the gifts and their purposes:

1. *Charismata*—grace gifts

There are diversities of gifts, but the same Spirit.
—I CORINTHIANS 12:4

2. *Diakonia*—ministry gifts

There are differences of ministries, but the same Lord.
—I CORINTHIANS 12:5

3. *Energemata*—supernatural gifts

And there are diversities of activities, but it is the same God who works all in all.

—1 CORINTHIANS 12:6

4. *Domata*—leadership gifts

And He Himself gave some to be apostles, some prophets, some evangelists, and some pastors and teachers, for the equipping of the saints for the work of ministry, for the edifying of the body of Christ, till we all come to the unity of the faith and of the knowledge of the Son of God, to a perfect man, to the measure of the stature of the fullness of Christ...

—EPHESIANS 4:11–13

These gifts are received and released in the church. Listen to one of the very first things Paul said to the Romans in his letter to them:

For I long to see you, that I may impart to you some spiritual gift, so that you may be established...

—ROMANS 1:11

And to Timothy, Paul's son in the faith:

Therefore I remind you to stir up the gift of God which is in you through the laying on of my hands.

—2 TIMOTHY 1:6

We're told in Romans 11:29 that these gifts and callings are irrevocable. Imagine it! God is willing to place a call on your life and gift you accordingly to fulfill it, and those things are binding and unchangeable.

My heart has not always been open to the supernatural gifts. Like so many others, I found it easy to relegate the more dramatic gifts to the first century. I find no scriptural support for the gifts having ceased. The only prooftext offered by those who oppose the present operation of spiritual gifts is in 1 Corinthians 13:8, "…tongues…will cease…" Obviously this points to the future when Christ shall come and there will be no more need of the gifts. Paul lists for us the supernatural gifts in 1 Corinthians 12:7–11:

> But the manifestation of the Spirit is given to each one for the profit of all: for to one is given the word of wisdom through the Spirit, to another the word of knowledge through the same Spirit, to another faith by the same Spirit, to another gifts of healings by the same Spirit, to another the working of miracles, to another prophecy, to another discerning of spirits, to another different kinds of tongues, to another the interpretation of tongues. But one and the same Spirit works all these things, distributing to each one individually as He wills.

God gives every believer a supernatural manifestation! The most common of these is tongues, but whatever the manifestation, God is willing to give it.

Gifts of Revelation

Word of wisdom

The word of wisdom releases practical counsel for daily living. It is supernaturally given as God's gift to provide answers to problems. We're told in James 3:15–17:

> This wisdom does not descend from above, but is earthly, sensual, demonic. For where envy and self-seeking exist, confusion and every evil thing are there. But the wisdom that is from above is first pure, then peaceable, gentle, willing to yield, full of mercy and good fruits, without partiality and without hypocrisy.

Word of knowledge

The word of knowledge releases information supernaturally given by God to a believer for others. Paul expounded on this in his letter to the Ephesians:

> …that the God of our Lord Jesus Christ, the Father of glory, may give to you the spirit of wisdom and revelation in the knowledge of Him, the eyes of your understanding being enlightened; that you may know what is the hope of His calling,

> what are the riches of the glory of His inheritance
> in the saints...
>
> —EPHESIANS 1:17–18

Discernment of spirits

Many see this gift simply as an ability to detect the presence of malevolent spirits. This is not the case. The discernment of spirits does give the ability to detect enemy spirits, but it is also intended to enable the bearer to read the spirit of other people. In Acts 8:23:

> For I see that you are poisoned by bitterness and
> bound by iniquity.

And in Acts 13:10:

> ...and said, "O full of all deceit and all fraud, you
> son of the devil, you enemy of all righteousness,
> will you not cease perverting the straight ways of
> the Lord?"

Gifts of Inspiration

The supernatural gifts function to inspire the believer using the gift, other believers, and oftentimes, unbelievers as well. These gifts and their explanations are listed here.

+ Prophecy—message from God in a known
  language or an interpretive tongue

+ Tongues—a supernatural utterance in a language not known to the speaker, either earthly or heavenly

+ Interpretation—the ability given by God to hear a language not known and understand it

Gifts of Operation

We have mentioned already that faith itself is a gift. But faith is more than just believing something. Faith is a supernatural ability to do extraordinary works. Faith has the ability to believe God without doubt or question, confesses the promise, and waits on its manifestation.

Gifts of Healing

This gift is, at once, simple to understand yet far-reaching in scope. Read Acts 10:38:

> How God anointed Jesus of Nazareth with the Holy Spirit and with power, who went about doing good and healing all who were oppressed by the devil, for God was with Him.

And read the great Messianic prophecy made in Isaiah 53:4–5:

> Surely He has borne our griefs and carried our sorrows; yet we esteemed Him stricken, smitten

by God, and afflicted. But He was wounded for
our transgressions, He was bruised for our iniqui-
ties; the chastisement for our peace was upon Him,
and by His stripes we are healed.

This gift is the ability to heal human sickness, to give
insight on the cause of sickness, and to give advice on treat-
ment as well as praying for the sick. Also this gift exists to
enable the believer to cast out demons of infirmity.

The purposes of healing are many.

- It authenticates the gospel message.
- It comforts and brings health to show God's
  mercy.
- It equips for service as impediments to
  ministry are removed.
- It brings glory to God.
- It shows God's love for mankind.
- It demonstrates the power and sovereignty
  of God.

Methods used in healing were many. Jesus laid hands
on people and everyone was healed. (See Matthew 9:18;
Luke 4:40.) Jesus primarily used this method. Note that
most often people didn't ask Jesus to pray for them in any
kind of general way, but they asked for healing.

Another symbol of Holy Spirit power for healing was
anointing with oil (Mark 6:13). James encourages:

> Is any among you sick? Let him call for the elders of the church and let them pray over him, anointing him with oil in the name of the Lord. And the prayer of faith will save the sick, and the Lord will raise him up. And if he has committed sins, he will be forgiven.
>
> —James 5:14–15

The New Testament emphasizes the faith of the sick person, also the faith of other people (paralytic lowered through the roof by four friends—Mark 2:3–12). The faith of others and praying as James did can release healing when the elders pray. It is their faith that releases the healing for another. For any of this we must have faith in Jesus! He is *Jehovah Rapha*, our Healer.

Gift of Miracles

The power of God enables a human being to release the miracle work and power of God. It is an ability given by God to contradict the laws of the natural world, to break the dimensional barrier between this world and the world to come.

CHAPTER EIGHT
The Miraculous Gifts
of the Holy Spirit

I N I Corinthians 12:10, we have the plural "workings of miracles" (*energemata dunameon*), which refers to extraordinary manifestations and can include healings. Usually this is associated with the mighty works of God apart from miracles of healing. Paul listed these as separate gifts. Miracles are associated with power, and this power far exceeds what man can do. The workings of miracles are an invasion against the kingdom of Satan and a sign of the breaking in of God's kingdom into this present world. The Greek word is *dunamis*, from which we get *dynamite*. The first miracle is salvation. Read Romans 1:16:

> For I am not ashamed of the gospel of Christ, for it is the power of God to salvation for everyone who believes, for the Jew first and also for the Greek.

The word *power* is "miracle" power (*dunamis*).

Miracles represent a whole other arena of opportunity for the eternal world to invade this world.

A miracle is a dimensional interruption! This miracle enables events to occur that normally could not without a reversal of natural law.

Miracles in Scripture

Paul afflicted Elymas, a magician, with blindness in Acts 13:11–12:

> And immediately a dark mist fell on him, and he went around seeking someone to lead him by the hand. Then the proconsul believed, when he saw what had been done, being astonished at the teaching of the Lord.

Recall other amazing miracles that God wrought for His glory.

- Bringing the dead back to life (Acts 9:6–42)
- God allowed the sun to stand still for Joshua to continue the battle (Josh. 10:1–15).

The miracles of Elijah in 1 Kings 17:1–16:

- Rain was withheld for three years.
- Elijah went to heaven in a chariot of fire.

The miracles of Jesus:

- Feeding of the five thousand by Jesus
- Water turned to wine
- Calming the storm
- Walking on the water

Miracles cause wonderment about God. A miracle is an event or action that contradicts scientific laws and goes beyond them by the acts of God. Miracles are displayed as signs and wonders.

The Purpose of Miracles

Miracles reveal the glory of God and demonstrate His power and love. Additionally, miracles minister to those who know nothing of Jesus. Miracles destroy the works of the enemy, and, most wondrously, they terrorize Satan! But can miracles be performed by common believers? Jesus said in John 14:12–14:

> Most assuredly, I say to you, he who believes in Me, the works that I do he will do also; and greater works than these he will do, because I go to My Father. And whatever you ask in My name, that I will do, that the Father may be glorified in the Son. If you ask anything in My name, I will do it.

Jesus began His ministry with a miracle—the turning of water into wine (John 2:1–11). He ended His ministry with a miracle—the ascension at Bethany (Acts 1:9–11). The Holy Spirit is here today to enrich the church body with gifts and miracles always affirming the gospel.

People are more afraid of the supernatural than they are their problems. They are more afraid of the supernatural than they are their sickness and their situations.

The Scripture teaches that without faith it is impossible to please God.

The church will not fail for lack of power. It may fail for refusing to recognize or use the power God has given us.

The Anointing for the Impossible

In 1 John 2:15–17 we are taught, clearly, that this world and its challenges are passing away:

> Do not love the world or the things in the world. If anyone loves the world, the love of the Father is not in him. For all that is in the world—the lust of the flesh, the lust of the eyes, and the pride of life—is not of the Father but is of the world. And the world is passing away, and the lust of it; but he who does the will of God abides forever.

We are told, further, that this is the last hour:

> Little children, it is the last hour; and as you have heard that the Antichrist is coming, even now many antichrists have come, by which we know that it is the last hour.
>
> —1 JOHN 2:18

The last hour will be characterized by religion with and against Christ. Christ means "anointed one"! Satan opposes the anointed body of Christ, the church, just as we read in 1 John 2:19:

> They went out from us, but they were not of us;
> for if they had been of us, they would have con-
> tinued with us; but they went out that they might
> be made manifest, that none of them were of us.

Wonderfully, there is an anointing that taps into the knowledge of the other world! As John wrote in 1 John 2:26–27:

> These things I have written to you concerning
> those who try to deceive you. But the anointing
> which you have received from Him abides in you,
> and you do not need that anyone teach you; but
> as the same anointing teaches you concerning all
> things, and is true, and is not a lie, and just as it
> has taught you, you will abide in Him.

Do not be deceived. There are gifts God can give you that cannot be taught but will operate in those who abide in Christ.

Bill Bright told the true story of the Yates' pool in West Texas. Mr. Yates lived the life of a pauper living on government subsidies and worrying constantly about providing for his family. He grazed sheep, and later in his life, a company approached him to drill for oil on his land.

They drilled 1,115 feet—hit 80,000 barrels—and some strikes were twice that. Thirty years later 125,000 barrels a day pumped from Yates' land.

He had owned the oil all that time. We, like that, live

in a spiritual poverty and don't realize our inheritance. The gifts are within us. Begin the journey of faith. Allow the gifts to flow in your life.

CHAPTER NINE
Welcoming the Gifts of the Holy Spirit

WHY ARE THE gifts not operating in all churches? The answer to that question must begin with the truth. The gifts are simply not welcome in all churches. The Holy Spirit will not force His gifts on any church. It is clear that the church without the gifts is impoverished and weakened. The gifts must be welcomed.

The gifts are not welcomed in some churches because of ignorance or incomplete teaching. This was true in my ministry for many years. I received teaching on the seven service gifts in Romans 12, yet I stayed away from the more sensational gifts because I had been convinced that these had ceased.

That all abruptly changed when I received the baptism with the Holy Spirit. Suddenly the supernatural world opened to me, and I came alive to the spiritual world. Soon angels were soaring into my life, demons were opposing my progress, and gifts were being released in my life. Across the years, God taught me the gifts and their blessings.

My question at that juncture was how do I move this traditional church to embrace the gifts? I soon learned it was as much about environment as education. There must be an atmosphere as well as spiritual instruction!

First, the gifts operate in an atmosphere of faith. Romans 12:6 reveals that the gifts operate in proportion to our faith. The power of the operation of the gifts is increased as faith is enlarged. Faith is believing what God has decreed in His Word is so, when it does not seem so, until it is so. Faith must speak the Word and believe on it for the gifts to be effective.

Second, there needs to be a spirit of expectation in the gathering. An atmosphere of anticipation will make way for the operation of the gifts. Before Paul journeyed to Rome, he set an expectation about releasing the gifts in his letter to them.

> First, I thank my God through Jesus Christ for you all, that your faith is spoken of throughout the whole world. For God is my witness, whom I serve with my spirit in the gospel of His Son, that without ceasing I make mention of you always in my prayers, making request if, by some means, now at last I may find a way in the will of God to come to you. For I long to see you, that I may impart to you some spiritual gift, so that you may be established—that is, that I may be encouraged together with you by the mutual faith both of you and me....
>
> But I know that when I come to you, I shall

> come in the fullness of the blessing of the gospel
> of Christ.
>
> —ROMANS 1:8–12; 15:29

Third, the church must be saturated with an atmosphere of genuine worship. The fullness of the Holy Spirit releases powerful singing in the Holy Spirit. This is not about music style, for Paul listened to every kind of music.

> And do not be drunk with wine, in which is dissipation; but be filled with the Spirit, speaking to one another in psalms and hymns and spiritual songs, singing and making melody in your heart to the Lord, giving thanks always for all things to God the Father in the name of our Lord Jesus Christ…
>
> —EPHESIANS 5:18–20

How do psalms, hymns, and spiritual songs promote melody and harmony? When worship flows in the anointing of the Holy Spirit, the atmosphere is changed for the supernatural gifting.

In the home of Cornelius while Jesus was being exalted in worship and preaching, the Holy Spirit released the gift of tongues. This manifestation of the gifts became a part of the Gentile Pentecost in Acts 10:44–46:

> While Peter was still speaking these words, the Holy Spirit fell upon all those who heard the word. And those of the circumcision who believed were astonished, as many as came with Peter, because

> the gift of the Holy Spirit had been poured out on
> the Gentiles also. For they heard them speak with
> tongues and magnify God.

God's Spirit is not limited by location, but He can certainly saturate a location.

Fourth, honoring God's gifted leaders can release the gifts. God often uses the ministry of anointed men and women who move in the gifts to release them on others. My wife, Paulette, was baptized in the Holy Spirit and received the gift of tongues some days after receiving ministry and the laying on of hands from Pastor Jack Hayford. The gifts can be imparted by the laying on of hands, as happened with Timothy, Paul's son in the faith.

Fifth, spiritual gifts are released in the unity of the gathered church for ministry. One of the appalling scandals in the church is how the use of gifts has become divisive. In Ephesians 4:11–13, we see clearly that the gifts were given to bring maturity and unity to the body.

> And He Himself gave some to be apostles, some
> prophets, some evangelists, and some pastors and
> teachers, for the equipping of the saints for the
> work of ministry, for the edifying of the body of
> Christ, till we all come to the unity of the faith and
> of the knowledge of the Son of God, to a perfect
> man, to the measure of the stature of the fullness
> of Christ.

As gifted members find their place in the church and connect with others, a powerful release of God's supply takes places.

> ...from whom the whole body, joined and knit together by what every joint supplies, according to the effective working by which every part does its share, causes growth of the body for the edifying of itself in love.
>
> —Ephesians 4:16

Churches must celebrate the diversity of gifts while embracing unity in the body! However, a church's motives must be right for the gifts to operate. Our basic desire must be to lead others to be fully developed followers of Jesus Christ; nothing less than the transformation of lives can be the goal. Our motive has to move beyond the desire for some kind of exciting gathering to the maturity of leading people to be overwhelmed and overtaken by the Lord Jesus Christ. When the true church gathers and glorifies the Lord Jesus Christ, He will deliver on His promise to give us all we need. Our motive must be soaked in love. We can have all the gifts and live beneath our privilege and dishonor Christ. Gifts remain when character leaves.

One can have the gifts, noise, and hoopla of charismatic gifting yet not serve people in love, and all it becomes is noise.

Though I speak with the tongues of men and of angels, but have not love, I have become sounding brass or a clanging cymbal. And though I have the gift of prophecy, and understand all mysteries and all knowledge, and though I have all faith, so that I could remove mountains, but have not love, I am nothing. And though I bestow all my goods to feed the poor, and though I give my body to be burned, but have not love, it profits me nothing.

—1 CORINTHIANS 13:1–3

Gifts without the right goals are worthless. Gifts neglected, wasted, abused, and buried are tragic indeed.

Let us welcome and worship the Giver of all gifts, the Holy Spirit of our Lord Jesus Christ.

CHAPTER TEN
Activating the Gifts of the Holy Spirit

O N MANY OCCASIONS I have had the privilege of praying over individuals to receive the baptism with the Holy Spirit and His gifts. I have watched as people will get a strained look on their faces. I want to say to them, "No, you are not trying to lay an egg!" Gifts by their very nature cannot be earned.

In order to activate the gifts of the Spirit, we must look again at the great word *charismata*. Its root word is *grace*! The charismata are "grace gifts." The gifts are not religious merit badges one earns by his own efforts. Rather, the gifts are God's endowment by the Holy Spirit to energize and enable kingdom work to be done through you.

> For by grace you have been saved through faith, and that not of yourselves; it is the gift of God, not of works, lest anyone should boast. For we are His workmanship, created in Christ Jesus for good works, which God prepared beforehand that we should walk in them.
>
> —EPHESIANS 2:8–10

The gifts of faith empower us and allow God to fashion us into new people. The word *workmanship* is translated from the Greek word *poiema*, from which our English word *poem* is derived.

The presence of the Holy Spirit takes all the clutter and confusion of life and artfully, by the gifts of the Spirit, transforms your life into an epic poem! Therefore, a church embracing the gifts must begin in an understanding of God's grace that freely offers His gifts to those who believe.

Second, to activate the gifts one must acknowledge the Holy Spirit's work in today's world. Gifts are only available to those who are not afraid to discover and open them. Several months before my wife's birthday I bought her a new leather-bound Bible. I put it away to hide it from her until the appropriate day. Subsequently I bought her other gifts, and we took a trip overseas to celebrate. I forgot the Bible I had purchased! Over a month later she found the package hidden in a cabinet. She asked me, "Ron, what is this?" Immediately I realized it was the gift! To her delight it was that Bible she wanted! The gift was there all the time, it was paid for, yet it had to be discovered and opened in order to be enjoyed!

The church life is a journey of revelation, blessing, and pursuit of deeper intimacy with God. That would be the third key to activating the gifts of the Spirit, a hunger for and a pursuit of God and His kingdom. This pursuit rises out of a hunger and thirst for the Word that draws us even closer to Him. The closer our proximity to Jesus, the more grace and gifting we receive.

The fourth key is a regular, passionate prayer life. God's "gifts" are available to those who ask, seek, and knock. (See Luke 11:5–13.) Your Father God loves you and desires to equip you for a life that is "much more." Through the merits of Jesus Christ and His cross God desires to give us freely that which we need.

Furthermore, we can activate the gifts by connecting with a local church where they believe, teach, and release the gifts of the Spirit! It is unlikely you will discover your gifts of the Spirit without being connected to a growing, worshiping, Spirit-anointed church. The Holy Spirit creates an atmosphere in the worship that removes our fear and inhibitions.

Motive is also important in activating the gifts of the Spirit. In Acts 8:14–24 we read the story of Simon the sorcerer who tried to buy the gift of the Holy Spirit. Peter discerned that his heart was not right with God and that he was bound by a spirit of bitterness. God's gifts will not operate in our lives if we are not in a right relationship with the Lord. Also, our motives cannot be personal gain or self-promotion. The gifts are given for the purpose of serving others in the community of faith and reaching those who need Christ.

Finally, let me add that those to whom God will give gifts must be flexible and available to do what God commands. Why would God activate a gift if you are unwilling to operate in that gift? I think of the deacon Philip who was willing to leave a mighty revival in Samaria in order to reach one African, a eunuch from Ethiopia. Those whom God gifts are expected to use those gifts to go wherever God may direct!

Anyone who has ever ordered a credit card has had to "activate" the card. Usually there is a toll-free number one calls, answers some questions, and then the card becomes useful. One can possess a card and never be able to enjoy its convenience without activating it. Also, if one violates the regulations on the card or does not pay, the card can be deactivated!

The gifts of the Spirit are given freely and are available to all. Yet they must be activated and remain activated, or they are useless.

Why not ask your heavenly Father right now to reveal and release His gifts in your life?

CHAPTER ELEVEN
The Last Days and the Gifts of the Spirit

Wᴇɴ ᴅɪꜱᴄᴜꜱꜱɪɴɢ ᴛʜᴇ gifts of the Spirit and the last days, there must be both excitement and caution! Let me begin by stating that the gifts of the Spirit's operation must increase in these last days! Notice the following truths in regard to gifting in the opening verses of 1 Corinthians:

> I thank my God always concerning you for the grace of God which was given to you by Christ Jesus, that you were enriched in everything by Him in all utterance and all knowledge, even as the testimony of Christ was confirmed in you, so that you come short in no gift, eagerly waiting for the revelation of our Lord Jesus Christ...
>
> —1 Cᴏʀɪɴᴛʜɪᴀɴꜱ 1:4–7

The great apostle acknowledges the riches and diversity of gifts operating in the Corinthian church. He acknowledges utterance gifts and discernment gifts are enriching the church. He further confirmed the presence of Jesus in their lives. Then Paul drops this statement that shatters any idea that the gifts have ceased.

Clearly the great apostle is concerned that the church not lag behind in the gifts of God as the second coming of Christ approaches. The word *revelation* is translated from the Greek word *apokalupsos*, which is referring to the unveiling of Christ at His second coming. Obviously Paul expected the operation of spiritual gifts to increase as the end draws near.

The gifts are said "to confirm" believers to "the end." The gifts also serve to purify the church in the last days, so that the church will be without blame.

The End Times church as described in Scripture seems to have a higher level of intensity than our current model. The parachurch today seems to embrace the belief that "less is more." There is an abandonment of the leadership of the Holy Spirit for a marketing plan that attracts people only through the five senses. While there is nothing wrong with using contemporary dress, music, and culture as vehicles to carry the gospel, it is not enough.

Many in the contemporary church have a back door through which members are exiting in search for a deeper relationship with God. This does not have to be so. The idea of "get it all done on Sunday" for an audience is not a New Testament plan for the church. Every member of the body is gifted and important. Therefore, the church of the last days must gather more often! (See Hebrews 10:25.)

Instead of fewer services, we are told the End Times church will gather more as she sees "the Day approaching."

Now these services must be alive with the Spirit of God and vibrant in worship.

As we approach the end of the age, the church faces greater challenges that can only be met by the enabling grace of God. The "stuff of this world" is not satisfying the inner hungers of the people. There is a spiritual thirst that only God's presence and gifting can quench.

Furthermore, there is a hunger for the supernatural world unlike anything I have experienced. The old gods of materialism and shallow entertainment are dying. The political systems have failed. The church increasingly lives in compromise and lukewarmness. The level of Western Christianity's commitment pales into a sick anemia compared to the blazing hot passion of a militant Muslim.

The spiritual awakening that is needed must include a renewal of the spiritual gifts of God! The gifts can and will facilitate a powerful breakthrough and allow God to direct His work through the church.

Some Cautions

The last days will also see a rise of counterfeit giftings released by the spirit of antichrist. As we're told in 2 Corinthians 11:13–15:

> For such are false apostles, deceitful workers, transforming themselves into apostles of Christ. And no wonder! For Satan himself transforms himself into an angel of light. Therefore it is no great thing if his ministers also transform themselves into ministers

of righteousness, whose end will be according to their works.

Satan will have counterfeit ministries who will imitate the gifts under demonic influence. There will be unleashed in the last days demonic leaders who will deceive and attempt to prostitute the things of God. Sadly, there will also be dead religion and churches that operate in the last days without the Spirit.

> But know this, that in the last days perilous times will come: For men will be lovers of themselves, lovers of money, boasters, proud, blasphemers, disobedient to parents, unthankful, unholy, unloving, unforgiving, slanderers, without self-control, brutal, despisers of good, traitors, headstrong, haughty, lovers of pleasure rather than lovers of God, having a form of godliness but denying its power. *And from such people turn away!*
> —2 TIMOTHY 3:1–5, EMPHASIS ADDED

This group will deny the gifts and power of the Holy Spirit. We are warned to "turn away" from such churches. All of this defection and deception is preparation to the coming of the Antichrist, whose spirit is now working in our world. (See 2 Thessalonians 2:9; 1 John 2:18.)

Satan and his demons are growing more active in these last days. Note that when the second beast, the false prophet, appears, he comes imitating the power of the Holy Spirit (Rev. 13:13–14).

So we must operate in the gifts and power of the Holy Spirit within the parameters of apostolic, prophetic, and pastoral coverings found in a local church. Also, we must abide in the truth of God's infallible Word. Finally, we must test supernatural gifts to see by what spirit they are operating. Believers are admonished in 1 John 4:1–3:

> Beloved, do not believe every spirit, but test the spirits, whether they are of God; because many false prophets have gone out into the world. By this you know the Spirit of God: Every spirit that confesses that Jesus Christ has come in the flesh is of God, and every spirit that does not confess that Jesus Christ has come in the flesh is not of God. And this is the spirit of the Antichrist, which you have heard was coming, and is now already in the world.

So let us celebrate and operate in the gifts. Let us embrace the authentic and reject the counterfeit. The miraculous and supernatural gifts of God are available to you today!

When my son was seven years old, he would take cookies from our pantry and offer them to the other kids in the neighborhood. One day when he was away with his mother, another little fellow knocked on my door. I looked down in the face of a seven-year-old boy. He looked up at me and said, "Give me a cookie." I said,

"Why should I give you a cookie?" He replied, "Because your son said you would." Wow! He got the cookie! Likewise, because God's Son said so, you can receive the supernatural gifts of the Spirit!

NOTES

Chapter 1
The Gifts of the Spirit: Their Need and Purpose

1. "Vote Recorder," The Thomas Edison Papers, http://edison.rutgers.edu/vote.htm (accessed November 7, 2011).

2. Creation was an act of the Trinity: God the Father willed it; God the Son created it by the power of God the Holy Spirit.

3. Wayne Grudem, *Systematic Theology* (Grand Rapids, MI: Zondervan, 1994), 634.

4. Thomas Scott, Matthew Henry, and William Jenks, *The Comprehensive Commentary on the Holy Bible; Containing the Text According to the Authorized Version* (Philadelphia: J. B. Lippincott & Co., 1859), 311.

5. A. W. Tozer, *Tozer: The Mystery of the Holy Spirit* (Alachua, FL: Bridge-Logos, 2007).

Chapter 3
The Availability of the Gifts of the Spirit Today

1. Siegfried Shatzmann, *A Pauline Theology of the Charismata* (Peabody, MA: Hendrickson Publishing, 1989), 78.

2. Archibald Robertson and Alfred Plummer, *A Critical and Exegetical Commentary on the First Epistle to the Corinthians*, 2nd edition (Edinburgh: T & T Clark, n.d.), 297.

3. Ken Hemphill, *Mirror, Mirror on the Wall*, (Nashville: Broadman Press, 1992), 78–80.

4. See chapter 1 of *An Essential Guide to Speaking in Tongues* (Lake Mary, FL: Charisma House, 2011).

5. For a more thorough discussion, see my book *Awakened by the Spirit* (Nashville: Thomas Nelson Publishers, 1999).

6. Jon Mark Ruthven, "Can a Charismatic Theology Be Biblical," http://www.tffps.org/docs/Foundations%20for%20a%20Charismatic%20Theology.pdf (accessed November 15, 2011).

7. Henry C. Vedder, A *Short History of the Baptists* (Valley Forge, PA: Judson Press, 1967), 3–10.

8. Ibid., 9–10.

9. Thomas Armitage, *A History of the Baptists*, vol. 1 (New York: Bryan, Taylor & Co., 1886).

10. Vedder, A *Short History of the Baptists*, 119–125

11. W. A. Jarrell, *Baptist Church Perpetuity* (Fulton, KY; National Baptist Publishing House, 1904), 69.

12. Ibid.

13. Ibid.

14. Ibid., 73, citing Moeller from *Schaff-Herzog Encyclopedia*, vol. 2, 1562.

15. Ibid., citing Neander from *History of the Christian Church*, vol. 1, 518–19.

16. Ibid., 74, citing Thomas Armitage from *A History of the Baptists*, 175.

17. Ibid., 75, citing William R. Williams from *Lectures on Baptist History*, 129.

18. Ibid., 76, citing Moeller from *Schaff-Herzog Encyclopedia*, vol. 2, 1562.

19. As told in Vedder, A *Short History of the Baptists*, 137–156.

20. See histories of the Baptists and my book *Awakened by the Spirit*.

21. Ben M. Bogard, *Pillars of Orthodoxy or Defenders of the Faith* (Fulton, KY: National Baptist Publishing House, 1901), 436.

22. Obviously, Azusa was the coming out and separation point of those who believe in the gifts and the birthing of new

groups. As uncomfortable as it may be for Baptists, the Pentecostals see our heritage as a part of their history.

23. John A. Broadus, *Sermons and Addresses* (Baltimore: R. H. Woodward, 1890), 228–230.

24. Frank Bartleman, *Another Wave of Revival* (Springdale, PA: Whitaker House, 1982), 26.

25. For more information, visit the website of Global Research Institute at Fuller Theological Seminary at http://www.fuller.edu/academics/centers-and-institutes/center-for-missiological-research/global-research-institute.aspx (accessed November 16, 2011).

Chapter 4
The Need for Spiritual Gifts

1. David Ireland, *Activating the Gifts of the Holy Spirit* (New Kensington, PA: Whitaker House, 1992), 13–35.

Chapter 6
The Seven Service Gifts of the Holy Spirit

1. Martin Luther and Wilhelm Pauck, *Luther: Lectures on Romans* (Louisville, KY: Westminster John Knox Press, 2006), 336.

Fundamental Truths for the Spirit-Filled Believer

Find clear biblical answers about how the Holy Spirit can work in your life with The Foundation on the Holy Spirit series by Pastor Ron Phillips.

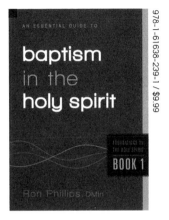

978-1-61638-239-1 / $9.99

978-1-61638-240-7 / $9.99

978-1-61638-492-0 / $9.99

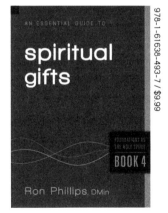

978-1-61638-493-7 / $9.99

10464